GCSE Mathematics 9-1
Target 9
Book 1

Barton Maths Tuition

ISBN: 9781723704024

GCSE questions targeted at level 9.

Barton Maths Tuition

This book is designed to provide students with an insight into how to tackle level 9 questions presented on the GCSE Mathematics Papers. The questions focus on strategy and technique rather than repetition as would normally be found in an exercise book.

The book is divided broadly into 10 exercises covering number, algebra, ratio, geometry, probability and statistics. Some questions require skills from several areas of GCSE mathematics. Questions labelled "**calculator**" may be solved with the use of any scientific calculator.

The questions are designed to stretch understanding of the harder topics on the exam.

These topics include:

1. Understanding variation.
2. Forming and solving relevant equations.
3. Linking algebra, geometry and probability interchangeably.

The full solutions are given at the end of each exercise. It is recommended that the solutions are studied carefully and that students take note of the methods used to solve the problems. There are 100 questions in the book. This book by itself will cover some, but not all, of the topics encountered on the GCSE syllabus. There will be other books available in the series that seek to cover the other topics.

CONTENTS

ACKNOWLEDGMENTS

The author wishes to thank Julia Sands for providing the illustrations and for editing this book.

Exercise 1

1 calculator

When we divide an integer by another integer that is not one of its factors we get a remainder. For example:

$$\frac{14}{3} = 4 \text{ remainder } 2$$

Find the values of a and b when:

$$\frac{163}{a} = 8 \text{ remainder } b \quad \text{and} \quad \frac{448}{a} = 23 \text{ remainder } b$$

2

(a)
A retail manager bought several items at a cost price of £x each.
The retail manager then added £8 to each item to form the selling price.
The retail manager sold some of the items for a total of £$4y$.
Write an expression in terms of x and y for the number of items sold.

(b)
The retail manager then sold the remaining items at £2 below the cost price.
The retail manager sold these remaining items for a total of £y.

Prove that the number of items bought originally was $\dfrac{5xy}{(x+8)(x-2)}$

3 calculator

Diesel prices fluctuate at a local garage.
One day a lorry driver finds the price has increased by 25%.
The driver can only afford to spend 10% more than normal on the fuel.
By what percentage will the volume of fuel purchased by the lorry driver be reduced?

4 calculator

A metal disc-shaped cylinder has a radius of 16cm and a depth of 1cm.
The density of the metal is 8g/cm³.
The mass of the disc is too large for its current purpose so a machine is used to cut cylindrical holes from the disc.
How many holes of radius 2cm would need to be cut out of the disc so that the density of the disc, including the space occupied by the holes, is 7g/cm³?

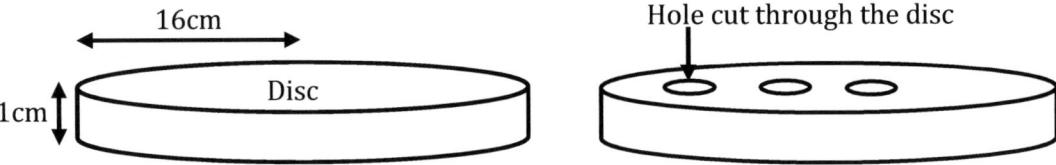

5 calculator

Some data was collected on the heights of garden walls.
The histogram below shows the data.
Data for the last two height intervals is missing.
There were as many walls below 90cm in height as there were walls between 90 and 140cm in height.
The interval between 130cm and 140cm in height made up $\frac{5}{34}$ of the total number of walls.
There are between 650 and 700 garden walls altogether.
Complete the histogram for the last two intervals and the units of the frequency density axis.

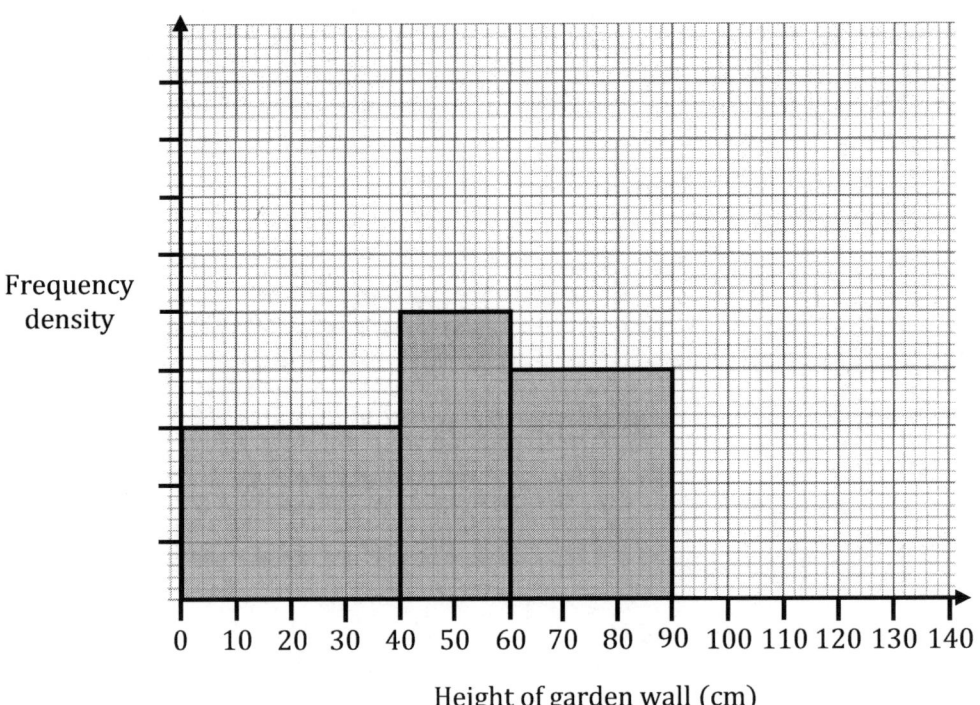

Height of garden wall (cm)

6

Find the lowest common multiple of $x^3 - 4xy^2$ and $x^2 - 2xy$.

7 calculator

A student collected some data on the ages of 170 people using a swimming pool.
The student drew a histogram for the data but unfortunately the paper fell in some water and some of the information was lost.
The data that could be recovered is shown on the histogram below.
The interval for 25 to 30 years has a frequency density of x.
The last interval was from 30 to y years and this interval had a frequency density one-eighth that of the 25 to 30 years representing 25 people.
It is unknown what age y represented.
Find the values of x and y.

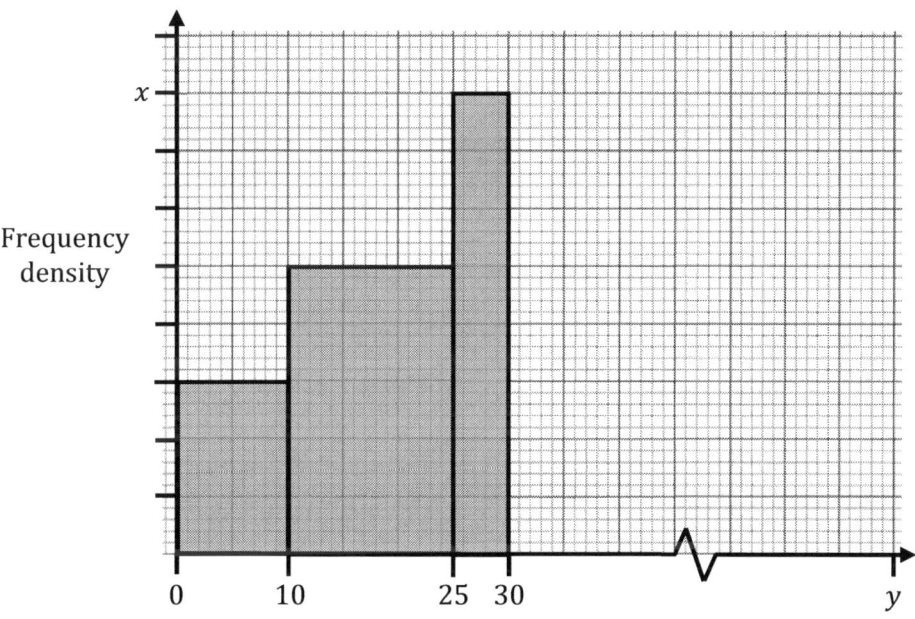

Age of people at swimming pool

8

$ABCD$ is a parallelogram.
AE and BE are straight lines.
Show that the area of triangle ABE is half the area of parallelogram $ABCD$.

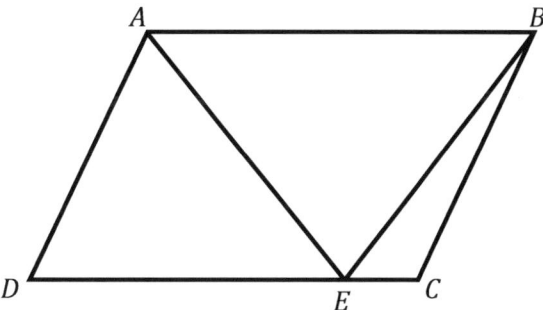

9 calculator

The diagram shows a trapezium $ABCD$.
The area of $ABCD$ is 60cm².
Angle $ABD = 30°$
$AB = 8$cm
$DC = 12$cm
$BC = x$cm
Find the value of x correct to three significant figures.

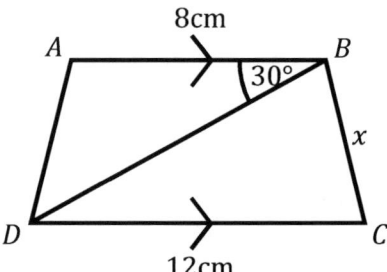

Not to scale

10 calculator

Two concerts are held.
Tickets for the first concert cost £x.
The total receipts for the first concert total £22,500.
The price of tickets for the second concert is reduced by £5 and 300 more tickets are sold.
The total receipts for the second concert increase by £11,250.
Find the value of x.

Exercise 1 Solutions

1

An integer can be written as the product of two integers in addition to a remainder.
The example hints at how we can relate the different values.
From $\frac{14}{3} = 4$ remainder 2 we can write:

$$4 \times 3 + 2 = 14$$

Using this with the given question we can write:
$8a + b = 163 \quad [1] \quad$ and $\quad 23a + b = 448 \quad [2]$

We have a pair of simultaneous equations to solve.

Subtracting [1] from [2] we obtain:
$15a = 285$
$\quad a = 19$

$$\begin{array}{r} 23a + b = 448 \quad [2] \\ -\quad 8a + b = 163 \quad [1] \\ \hline 15a = 285 \\ a = 19 \end{array}$$

Substituting $a = 19$ into equation [1]:
$8(19) + b = 163$
$\quad 152 + b = 163$
$\qquad\quad b = 11$

The correct answers are $a = 19$ and $b = 11$

2(a)

This question requires you to use algebra to represent each of the variables.
Often questions tell you a variable to use, say x, but sometimes you need to make up your own to answer the question.
Always remember with algebra that the letters will behave exactly the same way as if they were numbers.
This can help you link the given variables to form expressions and equations.
Since the information given in this question is algebraic, we can represent it in a table.

	Cost price (£)	Selling price (£)	Number of items sold	Total received (£)
Item	x	$x + 8$	n	$n(x + 8)$
				$4y$

We want an expression for the number of items sold; we will call this quantity n.
The total amount received can be written as two expressions which must be equal.
The first is to multiply the number of items sold by the selling price: $n(x + 8)$
The second is already given in the question: $4y$
Since these expressions are equal we can form an equation and make n the subject since this represents the number of items sold:

$$n(x + 8) = 4y$$
$$n = \frac{4y}{x + 8} \qquad \text{Divide by } (x + 8).$$

The expression required is $\frac{4y}{x+8}$.

2(b)

We can continue to add information to the table to help form the expression required.

	Remaining items	Selling price (£)	Number of items sold	Total received (£)
Item	m	$x - 2$	m	$m(x - 2)$
				y

Call the remaining unsold items m.
From this we know that the sum $n + m$ is the number of items bought originally.
First we make m the subject:

$$m(x - 2) = y$$
$$m = \frac{y}{x - 2}$$

Now we form the expression for the number of items bought originally:

$$n + m = \frac{4y}{x + 8} + \frac{y}{x - 2}$$
$$= \frac{4y(x - 2) + y(x + 8)}{(x + 8)(x - 2)}$$
$$= \frac{4xy - 8y + xy + 8y}{(x + 8)(x - 2)}$$
$$= \frac{5xy}{(x + 8)(x - 2)}$$

Combine the fractions into a common denominator:
$$\frac{4y}{x + 8} + \frac{y}{x - 2} = \frac{4y(x - 2) + y(x + 8)}{(x + 8)(x - 2)}$$
Expand the brackets.
Simplify.

This is the expression required.

3

This question can be solved using algebra.
We can represent the variables in a table.
Call the original cost per litre x pounds per litre.
Call the amount normally purchased y litres.
The total amount spent will be xy pounds.
Note the product of the first two columns equals the third column in the table.

Price per litre (£/litre)	Amount purchased (litres)	Total spend (£)
x	y	xy
$1.25x$	$0.88y$	$1.1xy$

The cost has increased by 25%, so the price per litre will be $1.25x$.
The multiplier 1.25 increases a value by 25%.
The new amount that the driver can spend is $1.1xy$ since the driver can afford to spend 10% more.
The multiplier 1.1 increases a value by 10%.
To find the amount that can be purchased now we divide the total spend by the price per litre:
$$\text{new amount purchased} = \frac{1.1xy}{1.25x}$$
$$= 0.88y$$

0.88 is the multiplier for a 12% reduction.
The correct answer is 12%.

4

The density formula required for this question is: density $= \dfrac{\text{mass}}{\text{volume}}$

As always with formulae, make sure your units are consistent.
The question used g/cm^3, so the mass will be in grams and the volume in cubic centimetres.
The overall volume being considered does not vary; it will still be a cylinder of radius 16cm and depth 1cm.
What will be changing is the mass of the cylinder.
This must change since the density has reduced from 8 to 7g/cm^3.
The unknown variable is the number of cylindrical holes which need to be removed.
We can call this number n.
We can now form an equation involving n and solve it:

$$\text{density} = \frac{\text{mass of original cylinder} - n \times \text{mass of each cylinder removed}}{\text{volume of original cylinder}}$$

The density is 7g/cm^3.
The volume of the original cylinder can be found by using the volume of a cylinder formula:

$$\begin{aligned}\text{volume of cylinder} &= \pi r^2 h \\ &= \pi \times 16^2 \times 1 \\ &= 256\pi\end{aligned}$$

The mass of the original cylinder can be found using the density formula:

$$\text{density} = \frac{\text{mass}}{\text{volume}}$$
$$\begin{aligned}\text{mass} &= \text{density} \times \text{volume} \\ &= 8 \times 256\pi \\ &= 2048\pi\end{aligned}$$

The volume of each cylinder removed will be:

$$\begin{aligned}\text{volume of cylinder} &= \pi r^2 h \\ &= \pi \times 2^2 \times 1 \\ &= 4\pi\end{aligned}$$

The mass of each cylinder removed will be:

$$\begin{aligned}\text{mass} &= \text{density} \times \text{volume} \\ &= 8 \times 4\pi \\ &= 32\pi\end{aligned}$$

We can now substitute all these values into the above equation:

$$\text{density} = \frac{\text{mass of original cylinder} - n \times \text{mass of each cylinder removed}}{\text{volume of original cylinder}}$$

$$\begin{aligned}7 &= \frac{2048\pi - n \times 32\pi}{256\pi} \\ &= \frac{2048 - 32n}{256} \\ 1792 &= 2048 - 32n \\ 32n &= 256 \\ n &= 8\end{aligned}$$

Cancel π from fraction.
Multiply by 256.
Add $32n$.
Subtract 1792.
Divide by 32.

The correct answer is 8.

5

Since the number of walls must be a whole number we can use the fact that there are between 650 and 700 walls to deduce exactly how many walls the histogram represents.

If you can write a fraction, $\frac{5}{34}$, of the total and obtain a whole number, then the total number must be a multiple of 34.

We can see that 680 is the only multiple of 34 between 650 and 700 (34×20).

There were 680 garden walls altogether.

$$\frac{5}{34} \text{ of } 680 = \frac{5}{34} \times 680$$
$$= 100$$

There were 100 walls between 130cm and 140cm.
We know that 90cm to 140cm represented half the 680 total.

$$\frac{680}{2} = 340$$

To find the number of walls between 90cm and 130cm we subtract 100:
$340 - 100 = 240$

There were 240 walls between 90cm and 130cm.
We can now calculate the frequency density for the last two intervals:

$$\text{frequency density} = \frac{\text{frequency}}{\text{class width}}$$
$$= \frac{100}{10}$$
$$= 10$$

The frequency density for 130cm to 140cm is 10.

$$\text{frequency density} = \frac{\text{frequency}}{\text{class width}}$$
$$= \frac{240}{40}$$
$$= 6$$

The frequency density for 90cm to 130cm is 6.
We know that the area of the rectangles in a histogram sum to the frequency.
We know that the area of walls with heights above 90cm must be equal to that below 90cm.
If we let one large square be one unit on the histogram we can say the area below 90cm is:

$$\text{area} = 3 \times 40 + 5 \times 20 + 4 \times 30$$
$$= 120 + 100 + 120$$
$$= 340$$

Notice that this total is identical to the total that the interval of 0cm to 90cm should be.
This means that the scale selected here is correct and that the frequency density axis increases by 1 unit for each large square.
The column for 130cm to 140cm is 10 units in height and the column for 90cm to 130cm is 6 units in height.

The completed histogram is shown below:

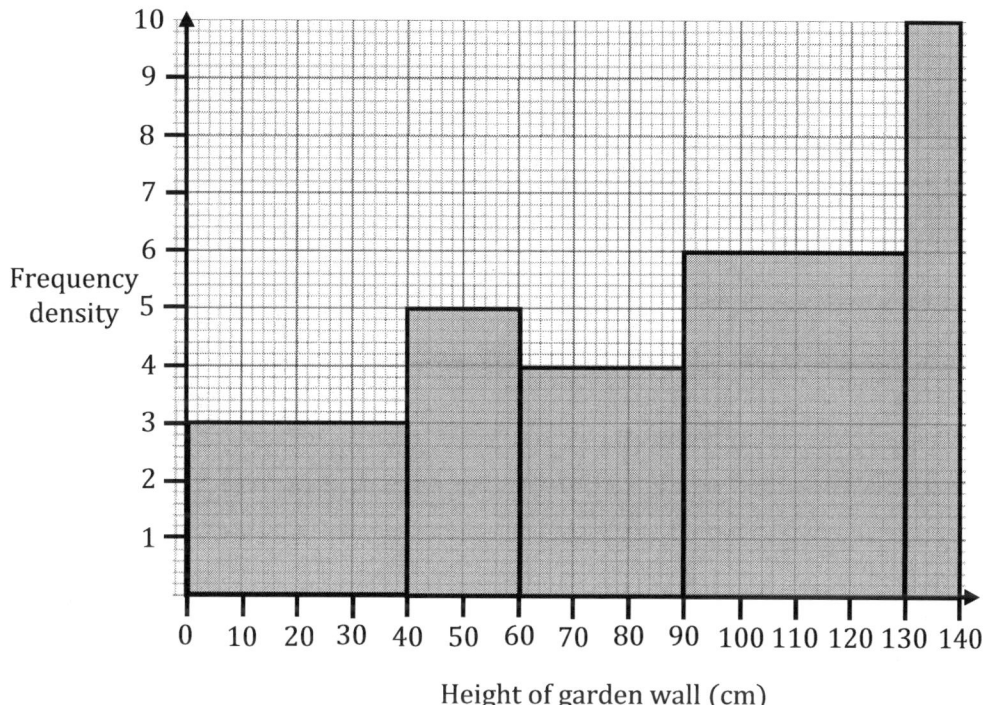

Height of garden wall (cm)

We know the units for the frequency density axis are 1, 2, 3 ...
A completed frequency table for the data is shown below.

Height of garden wall hcm	Frequency	Frequency Density
$0 < h \leq 40$	120	3
$40 < h \leq 60$	100	5
$60 < h \leq 90$	120	4
$90 < h \leq 130$	240	6
$130 < h \leq 140$	100	10

6

To find the lowest common multiple (LCM) we require the highest common factor (HCF) for each expression.
We obtain this by factorising fully each of the expressions:

$$x^3 - 4xy^2 = x(x^2 - 4y^2)$$ Factor x out.
$$= x(x + 2y)(x - 2y)$$ Notice the difference of two squares $a^2 - b^2 = (a + b)(a - b)$

$$x^2 - 2xy = x(x - 2y)$$ Factor x out

The highest common factor is found by checking for factor pairs.
We can see that x and $(x - 2y)$ is shared in both expressions.
Therefore the HCF is $x(x - 2y)$.

To find the LCM we multiply the HCF by the factors we did not pair: $(x + 2y)$

$\text{LCM} = x(x - 2y) \times (x + 2y)$

$\qquad = x(x + 2y)(x - 2y)$

$$x^3 - 4xy^2 = x \times (x - 2y) \times (x + 2y)$$
$$x^2 - 2xy = x \times (x - 2y)$$

The correct answer is $x(x + 2y)(x - 2y)$.
Alternative answer $x^3 - 4xy^2$.

Circle the shared factors: these tell you the HCF
Then multiply the shared factors by the non-shared factors to obtain the LCM.

7

We can start by writing the frequency density values in terms of x.
From the frequency densities we can write expressions for the frequencies of the known rectangles.
Remember that the frequency is equal to the area of each rectangle.
We are told the frequency density for the 30 to y year interval is one eighth of x.
This data can be displayed in a table:

Age interval	Frequency density	Frequency
0 – 10	$\dfrac{3}{8}x$	$10 \times \dfrac{3}{8}x = \dfrac{15}{4}x$
10 – 25	$\dfrac{5}{8}x$	$15 \times \dfrac{5}{8}x = \dfrac{75}{8}x$
25 – 30	x	$5 \times x = 5x$
30 – y	$\dfrac{1}{8}x$	$\dfrac{1}{8}x \times (y - 30) = 25$

We know the $30 - y$ interval represented 25 people, so we can form an equation containing x and y:

$\dfrac{1}{8}x(y - 30) = 25$ \qquad Multiply by 8.

$\quad x(y - 30) = 200$ [1]

We know the total frequency was 170, so we can form another equation containing x and solve:

$\dfrac{15}{4}x + \dfrac{75}{8}x + 5x + 25 = 170$

$\qquad \dfrac{145}{8}x + 25 = 170$ \qquad Collect the x terms.

$\qquad\qquad\qquad$ Subtract 25.

$\qquad \dfrac{145}{8}x = 145$ \qquad Multiply by 8.

$\qquad\qquad\qquad$ Divide by 145.

$\qquad\qquad x = 8$

We now substitute this value of x into equation [1]:

$8(y - 30) = 200$ \qquad Divide by 8.

$\quad y - 30 = 25$ \qquad Add 30.

$\qquad\quad y = 55$

The correct answer is $x = 8$ and $y = 55$

The completed histogram is shown below.

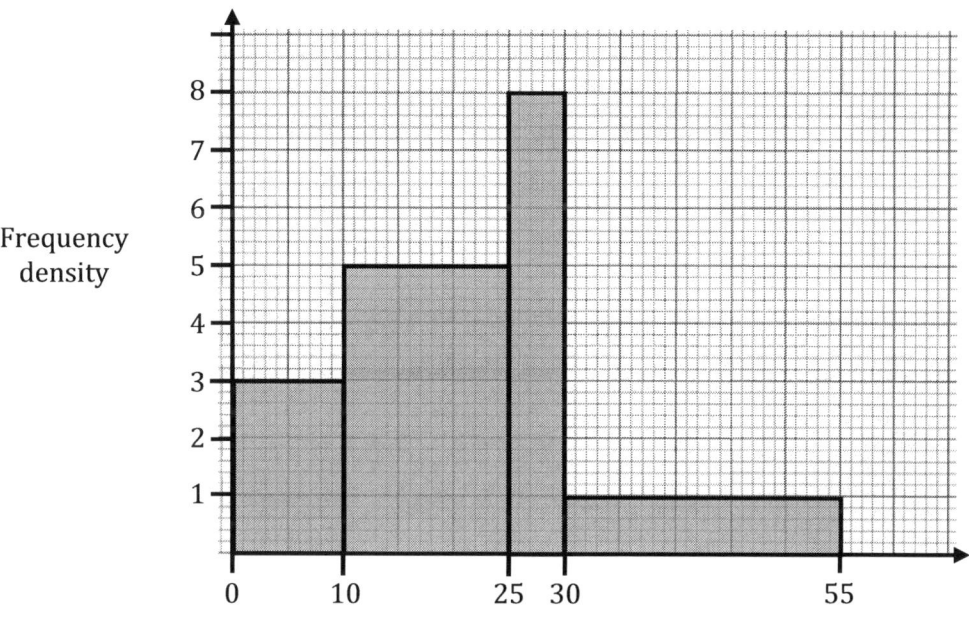

Frequency density

Age of people at swimming pool

8

Consider a line drawn from E and parallel to BC that joins AB at F.
The line would split the parallelogram $ABCD$ into two parallelograms $AFED$ and $FBCE$.
The line AE is a diagonal that splits $AFED$ in half.
The line BE is a diagonal that splits $FBCE$ in half.
The triangles AFE and BFE are equal in area to the triangles ADE and BEC respectively (congruent SSS).
Since the triangle ABE is formed from triangles AFE and BFE we can say it is half the area of the parallelogram.

The shaded area is half the area of the parallelogram.

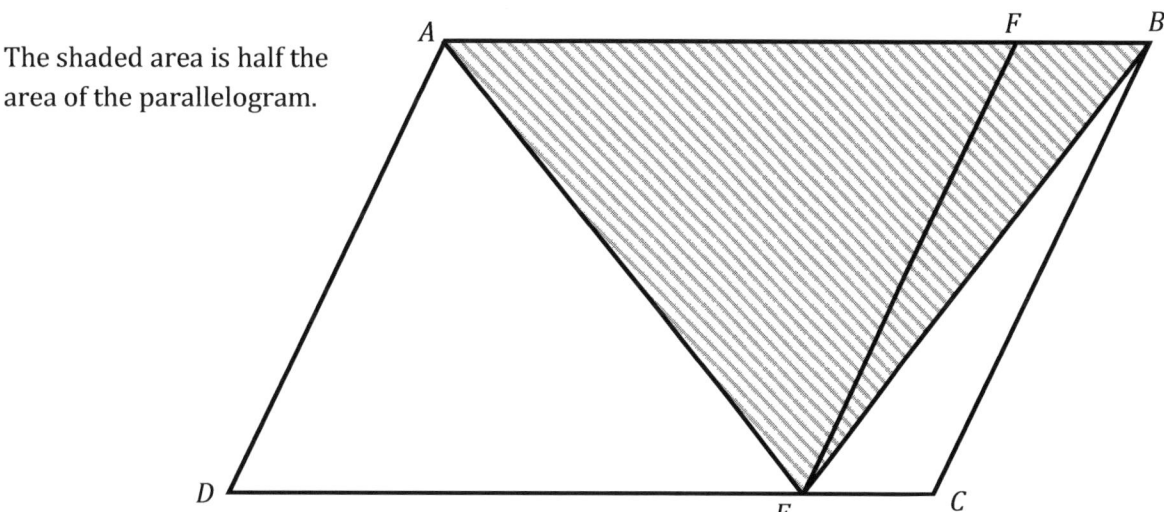

9

The area of a trapezium is given by the formula:

$$\text{area} = \frac{1}{2}h(a+b)$$

We already have a and b which are the parallel sides of 8 and 12cm.
Since we also have the area we can determine h, the height of the trapezium:

$$\frac{1}{2}h(a+b) = 60$$
$$\frac{1}{2}h(8+12) = 60$$
$$20h = 120$$
$$h = 6$$

Ideally we need to form a triangle that contains x as one of the sides.
Since the sides AB and DC are parallel we can say that angle $BDC = 30°$ since it is alternate to angle ABD.
We can draw a perpendicular line from B down to the line DC.
We will call the point where the perpendicular meets the line E.
The height of the triangle BDE will be the same as the height of the trapezium, 6cm.
We also know that the angles in this triangle will be $30°, 60°$ and $90°$.
We can use trigonometry to find the side DE:

$$\tan 60° = \frac{\text{opposite}}{\text{adjacent}}$$
$$= \frac{DE}{6}$$
$$DE = 6\tan 60°$$
$$= 6\sqrt{3}$$

We can now say that the side $EC = \left(12 - 6\sqrt{3}\right)$.
We now have enough information to use Pythagoras on the triangle BEC.

$$BC^2 = BE^2 + EC^2$$
$$x^2 = 6^2 + \left(12 - 6\sqrt{3}\right)^2$$
$$= 36 + \left(12 - 6\sqrt{3}\right)\left(12 - 6\sqrt{3}\right)$$
$$= 36 + 144 - 72\sqrt{3} - 72\sqrt{3} + 108$$
$$= 288 - 144\sqrt{3}$$
$$x = 6.211 \ldots$$

Substitute the side lengths into the
Pythagorean relation $a^2 + b^2 = c^2$.
Expand the brackets.
Simplify.
Square root.

The correct answer is 6.21cm correct to three significant figures.
Note that it is also possible to calculate the length of side DB as 12cm using Pythagoras on triangle BDE.
You can then use the cosine rule to find x:
$$a^2 = b^2 + c^2 - 2bc\cos A$$
$$x^2 = 12^2 + 12^2 - 2 \times 12 \times 12 \cos 30°$$
$$= 144 + 144 - 288\cos 30°$$
$$= 38.58 \ldots$$
$$x = 6.211 \ldots$$

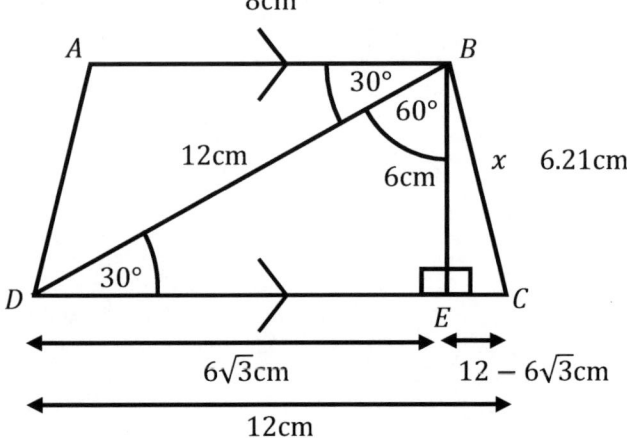

10

We can form a table showing the variables and how they alter after the £5 price reduction.
Note that the product of the price per ticket and the number of tickets sold is equal to the total receipts.
The total receipts increase by £11,250 after a £5 reduction.

Price per ticket	Number of tickets sold	Total receipts
x	$\dfrac{22500}{x}$	£22500
$x - 5$	$\dfrac{33750}{x - 5}$	£33750

Note that the number of tickets sold increased by 300.
This connection allows us to form and solve an equation for x:

number of tickets sold after = number of tickets sold before + 300

$$\frac{33750}{x - 5} = \frac{22500}{x} + 300$$

Multiply by $(x - 5)$.

$$33750 = \frac{22500(x - 5)}{x} + 300(x - 5)$$

Multiply by x.
Expand the brackets.

$$33750x = 22500(x - 5) + 300x(x - 5)$$

Simplify.

$$33750x = 22500x - 112500 + 300x^2 - 1500x$$

$$300x^2 - 12750x - 112500 = 0$$

Collect the terms on one side.

$$2x^2 - 85x - 750 = 0$$

Divide by 150.

$$(2x + 15)(x - 50) = 0$$

Factorise/ use quadratic formula.

$2x + 15 = 0$ is not a possible solution since $x > 0$.
The correct solution is $x = 50$.

Exercise 2

1 calculator

The diagram shows a trapezium $ABCD$.
A circle is drawn inside the trapezium.
The four sides of the trapezium form tangents to the circle.
The circle has an area of $16\pi\text{cm}^2$.
$AB = 6\text{cm}$
What is the area of the trapezium?

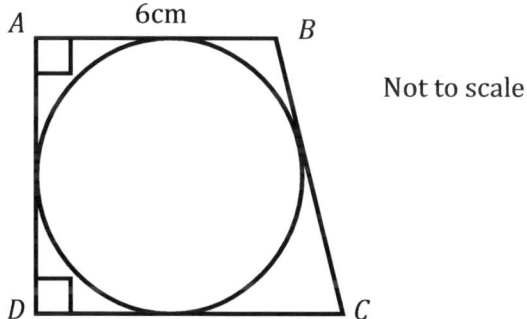

Not to scale

2

A population of fruitflies is increasing.

The population P of fruitflies at t days is modelled by the formula $P = k \times 4^{\frac{t}{3}}$ where k is a constant.
At x days the population is N.
Three days later the population has increased by 10800.
Find the value of N.

3 calculator

A man sets off from a point A at 1pm and walks at a constant speed of 4mph.
Two hours later a cyclist sets off from A travelling at 8mph in the same direction as the man.
The cyclist stops after one hour to repair a broken chain, taking two hours, before continuing at 16mph.
At what time does the cyclist overtake the man?

4

Some plates are stored in two different sizes of box.
The larger box holds 18 plates.
The smaller box holds 8 plates.
The total number of plates stored in the large boxes was four more than the total number stored in the small boxes.
There were 7 more small boxes than large.
All the boxes are full.
Find the total number of plates and the number of each type of box.

5 calculator

The two pie charts below show the mass composition of the known universe as percentages.
All values are given as a percentage.
The pie chart on the left shows the overall mass composition of the known universe.
The pie chart on the right shows the composition of the other 0.83%.
How many times more massive is the Dark energy component than the Heavy elements component?

Dark energy $(3x^2 - 4.83)\%$
Dark matter $x^2\%$
Hydrogen and helium $(x - 1)\%$
Other 0.83%

Percentages given out of known universe.
Stars $(17y - 0.01)\%$
Neutrinos $10y\%$
Heavy elements $y\%$

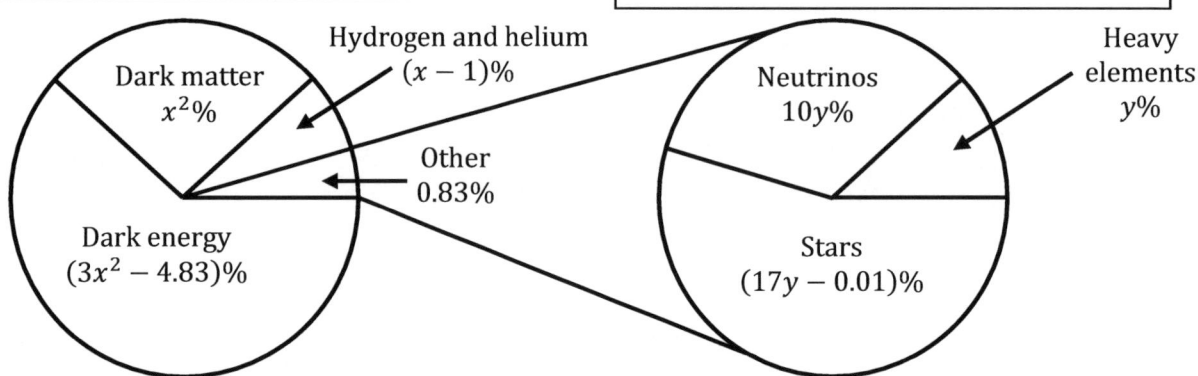

6 calculator

AD, AXC, BC and BXD are straight lines.
Angle $DAC = (x^2 + 15)°$
Angle $AXD = 16x°$
Angle $ADB = (14x - 10)°$
Angle $ACB = (2x^2 + 10)°$
Prove that the points A, B, C and D lie
on the circumference of the same circle.

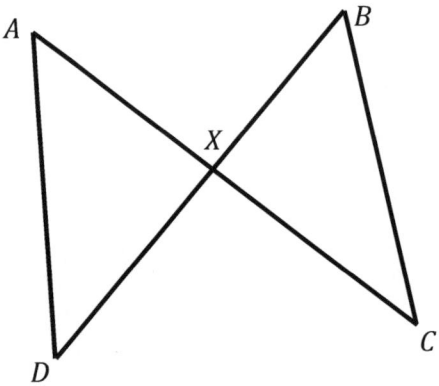

7 calculator

A cartographer is measuring the distances between hills.
He knows that the distance between the hills A and B is 21 miles.
The cartographer climbs to the top of Hill C where he determines the following:
Hill A is on a bearing of 330°.
Hill B is on a bearing of 030° and is 9 miles further away than Hill A.
How far away is Hill A from Hill C?

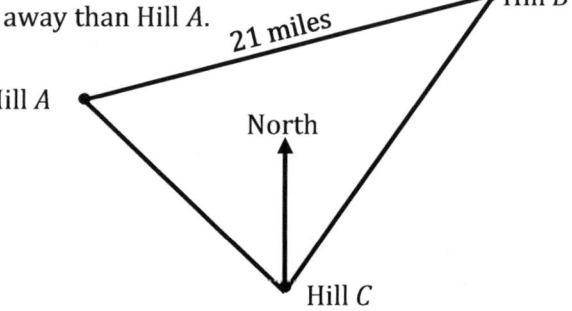

8 calculator

The two incomplete histograms below show the age distribution of 80 people in a village.
The histogram on the left shows the ages of the 80 people in 2012.
The histogram on the right shows the ages of the same 80 people 5 years later.
Both histograms are drawn to the same scale.
The oldest person in 2012 was 54.
Five years later, there are two more people in the $50 < a \leq 60$ category and eight less people in the $0 < a \leq 20$ category.
How many people were in the $20 < a \leq 50$ category in 2012?

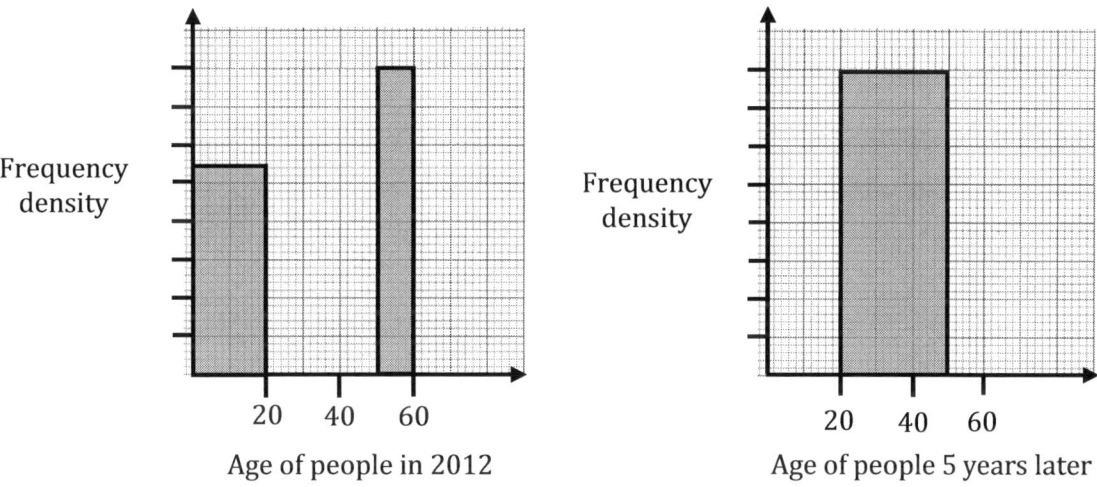

Frequency density — Age of people in 2012

Frequency density — Age of people 5 years later

9 calculator

x delivery drivers can deliver y packages in four hours.
If there are three more delivery drivers they can deliver 45 more packages in three and a half hours.
If a delivery driver can deliver 10 packages in one hour, find the values of x and y.

10 calculator

An arctic fox hunts for food in a climate with frequent snowfall.
The probability of snowfall on any given day is 0.6.
The probability of finding food changes depending on whether there has been a snowfall that day.
The probability of the arctic fox finding food on a given day is $\frac{59}{150}$.
The probability of the arctic fox finding food when there has been a snowfall is 10% less than the probability of not finding food when there has been no snowfall.
Find the probability of the arctic fox finding food after a snowfall.

Exercise 2 Solutions

1

We need to determine the height of the trapezium AD and the other parallel side length DC.

We already know the other parallel side AB is 6cm.

AD is the same as the diameter of the circle.

We are given the area of the circle so we can get the diameter:

$$\text{area} = \pi r^2$$
$$16\pi = \pi r^2$$
$$16 = r^2$$
$$r = 4$$

So the diameter is 8cm.

To calculate DC we need to examine the tangents to the circle and the significance of similar triangles.

We start by drawing a vertical line that runs parallel to AD and joins the points where the tangents touch the circles.

Call this line EF.

Call the centre of the circle O and draw three more lines.

The first line connects O and B.

The second line connects the centre O to the tangent BC at right angles (call this point G).

The third line connects the centre O to the point C.

In geometry, two tangents drawn from a point to a circle will have the same length.

This means $BE = BG$ and $CG = CF$.

We know $AE = 4$cm, so $EB = 2$cm because AE is the same as the radius.

$BG = 2$cm and $OG = 4$cm, again another radius.

An enlarged diagram of $EBCF$ is shown below.

The line OB splits the kite $OEBG$ in half so it splits the angle EOG in half.

This is shown by the angle x.

The line OC splits the kite $OGCF$ in half so it splits the angle FOG in half.

This is shown by the angle y.

We can say:

$$x + x + y + y = 180°$$
$$2x + 2y = 180°$$
$$2(x + y) = 180°$$
$$x + y = 90°$$

We can say angle $GOC = 90° - x$ which we have called y.

We can say angle $OBG = 90° - x$ which means that this angle is also equal to y.

This means the angle $OCG = x$ since its two other angles are $90°$ and y.

We have shown that the triangles OBG and OCG are similar.

The side of interest is FC since this is part of the other parallel side required for the area calculation.

This side is equal in length to CG.

Using similar triangles we can say:

$$\frac{CG}{4} = \frac{OG}{BG}$$
$$= \frac{4}{2}$$
$$CG = 8$$

So $FC = 8$cm

This means the overall length of the side DC is 12cm ($4 + 8$).
Now we can use the area of a trapezium formula:

$$\text{Area} = \frac{1}{2}h(a + b)$$
$$= \frac{1}{2} \times 8(6 + 12)$$
$$= 72$$

The correct answer is 72cm².

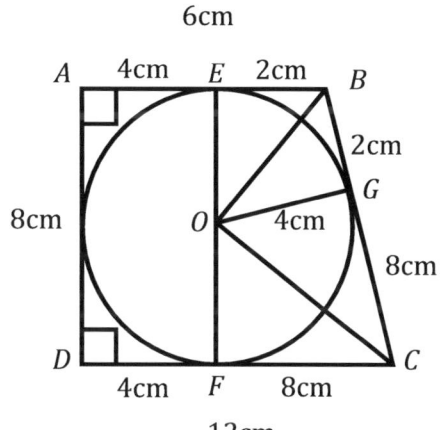

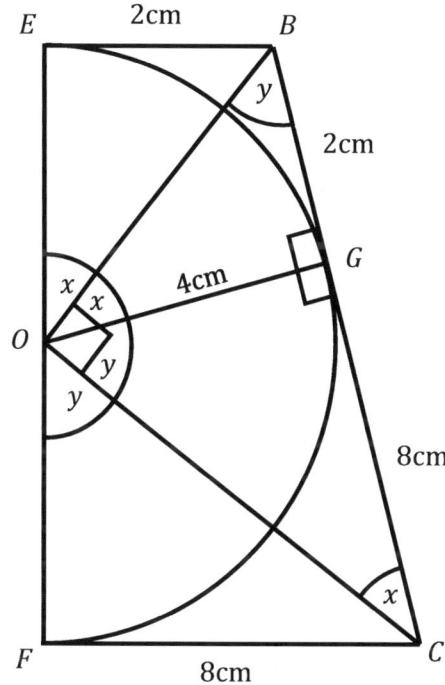

2

The question has provided two instances of the population at a given time.
We can form a pair of simultaneous equations to solve for N.
At x days the population is N:

$$P = k \times 4^{\frac{t}{3}}$$
$$N = k \times 4^{\frac{x}{3}} \quad [1]$$

Three days later the population has increased by 10800:

$$N + 10800 = k \times 4^{\frac{x+3}{3}} \quad [2]$$

It appears that we have two equations and three unknowns: N, x and k.
If we divide equation [1] by [2] we can eliminate k and x:

$$\frac{N}{N + 10800} = \frac{k \times 4^{\frac{x}{3}}}{k \times 4^{\frac{x+3}{3}}}$$

Divide the left hand side of [1] by the left hand side of [2].
Divide the right hand side of [1] by the right hand side of [2].

$$= \frac{4^{\frac{x}{3}}}{4^{\frac{x+3}{3}}}$$

Cancel the k.
Dividing numbers with the same base (4) means we subtract the powers.

$$= 4^{\frac{x}{3}-\left(\frac{x+3}{3}\right)}$$
$$= 4^{\frac{x}{3}-\left(\frac{x}{3}+1\right)}$$
$$= 4^{-1}$$
$$= \frac{1}{4}$$

$$\frac{x + 3}{3} = \frac{x}{3} + 1$$

Multiply out the powers in the brackets and simplify.

$$4^{-1} = \frac{1}{4}$$

$$N = \frac{1}{4}(N + 10800)$$
$$4N = N + 10800$$
$$3N = 10800$$
$$N = 3600$$

Multiply by $(N + 10800)$.
Multiply by 4.
Subtract N.
Divide by 3.

The correct answer is $N = 3600$.

3

This question can be represented on a distance-time graph.
We can plot a few key values from the information given.
The cyclist will overtake the man when the two lines meet.
We know that the man is walking for 2 hours at 4mph before the cyclist starts.
The man would have walked 8 miles in this time.
The cyclist starts at 3pm travelling for 1 hour at 8mph.
The cyclist has travelled 8miles at 4pm.
Then the cyclist is stationary for 2 hours while the chain is repaired, now 6pm.
The cyclist continues at 16mph for the rest of the journey until the man is overtaken.
It is this time we need to determine.
A sketch graph is shown below with key values added.

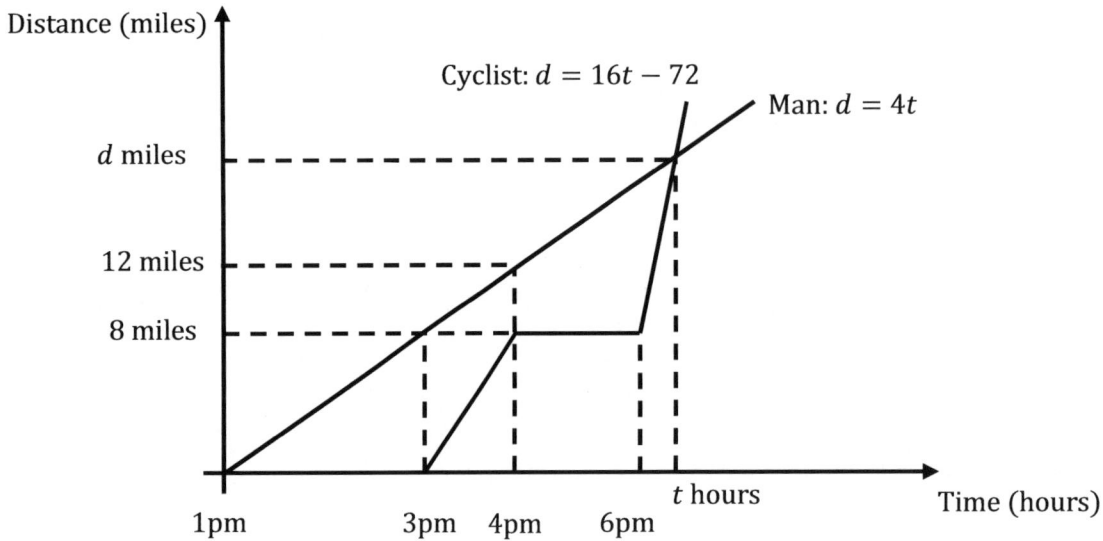

The gradient of a distance-time graph is the speed.
This means we can give an equation to the line shown for the man (1pm will be $t = 0$).
He travels d miles in t hours so the equation of this line will be $d = 4t$
Now we need an equation for the last line shown for the cyclist (the line when the cyclist travels at 16mph).
We know the gradient is 16 and we also know the coordinates $(5, 8)$ through which this line passes.
We can write an equation for the line in the form $y = mx + c$ where m is the gradient and c the distance axis intercept.

$y = mx + c$
$d = mt + c$ Replace y with d and x with t.
$8 = 16 \times 5 + c$ Substitute the coordinates $(5, 8)$ and the gradient 16 into the equation.
    $= 80 + c$ Subtract 80.
$c = -72$
$d = 16t - 72$

Now we find the point of intersection of $d = 4t$ and $d = 16t - 72$:
$16t - 72 = 4t$ Since both equations are equal to d the right hand side of each is set equal to each other.
$12t - 72 = 0$ Subtract $4t$
    $12t = 72$ Add 72.
      $t = 6$ Divide by 12.

This means the cyclist overtook the man at 7pm.

4

We can express the information given in a table.
Call the number of large boxes x.
Call the number of small boxes y.

	Plates per box	Number of boxes	Total plates
Large box	18	x	$18x$
Small box	8	y	$8y$

We can now link the variables in the table.
The total number of plates stored in the large boxes was four more than the total number stored in the small boxes.
$18x = 8y + 4$ [1]

There were 7 more small boxes than large.
$y = x + 7$ [2]

Substitute equation [2] into [1]:

$18x = 8(x + 7) + 4$	Substitute $y = x + 7$ into $18x = 8y + 4$
$= 8x + 56 + 4$	Expand the brackets.
$= 8x + 60$	Subtract $8x$.
$10x = 60$	Divide by 10.
$x = 6$	Substitute $x = 6$ into equation [2].
$y = 13$	

There are 212 plates altogether.
The table below shows the answer to the question.

	Number per box	Number of boxes	Total plates
Large box	18	6	108
Small box	8	13	104

5

The pie chart for the overall mass composition must sum to 100%.
We can form and solve an equation for x:

$3x^2 - 4.83 + x^2 + x - 1 + 0.83 = 100$	Set the expression sum equal to 100.
$4x^2 + x - 5 = 100$	Simplify the quadratic and set equal to zero.
$4x^2 + x - 105 = 0$	Factorise, accepting the positive solution only.
$(4x + 21)(x - 5) = 0$	

x must be positive so the correct solution is $x = 5$.
The pie chart identified as "other" must sum to 0.83%.
We can form and solve an equation for y:

$17y - 0.01 + 10y + y = 0.83$	Set the expression sum equal to 0.83.
$28y = 0.84$	Simplify.
$y = 0.03$	Add 0.01 and divide by 28.

We need to find how many times more massive the Dark energy component is than the Heavy elements component.

This is found by division:

$$\frac{\text{Dark energy}}{\text{Heavy elements}} = \frac{3x^2 - 4.83}{y}$$
$$= \frac{3(5)^2 - 4.83}{0.03}$$
$$= 2339$$

Component	Percentage
Dark energy	70.17
Dark matter	25
Hydrogen and helium	4
Stars	0.5
Neutrinos	0.3
Heavy elements	0.03

The correct answer is 2339.

6

The pattern of lines shown in the diagram are found when applying "angles in the same segment".
We must prove that angle DAC is equal to angle DBC, and angle ADB is equal to angle ACB.
We notice that the triangle AXD has all three of its angles defined in terms of x.
We know that the sum of these angles is $180°$.
We can form and solve an equation for x:

$$x^2 + 15 + 16x + 14x - 10 = 180 \qquad \text{Set the expressions equal to 180.}$$
$$x^2 + 30x - 175 = 0 \qquad \text{Simplify.}$$
$$(x + 35)(x - 5) = 0 \qquad \text{Set the quadratic equal to zero and factorise.}$$

x must be positive so the correct solution is $x = 5$.
We can now add the angles to the diagram.

$$x^2 + 15 = 5^2 + 15$$
$$= 40$$
$$16x = 16(5)$$
$$= 80$$
$$14x - 10 = 14(5) - 10$$
$$= 60$$
$$2x^2 + 10 = 2(5)^2 + 10$$
$$= 60$$

Angles in the same segment

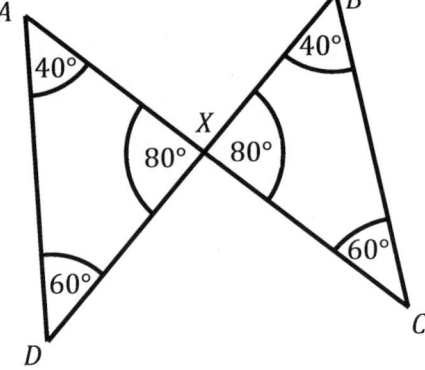

Angle AXD and angle BXC are opposite angles so are equal.
Angle DBC is $40°$ since there are $180°$ in a triangle.
We can see that the condition of "angles in the same segment" holds, therefore the points A, B, C and D all lie on the circumference of the same circle.

7

We can find the angle at Hill C from the information given.
Bearings are measured from North in a clockwise direction.

The bearing of Hill A from Hill C is $330°$ so the remaining part, $30°$, would go between the north at Hill C and the line connecting Hill A and C.
The bearing of Hill B from Hill C is $030°$ so this forms the angle between the north at Hill C and the line connecting Hill B and C.

Call the distance from Hill A to Hill C x miles.
Since the distance from Hill B to Hill C is 9 miles further we can call this distance $(x + 9)$ miles.
We have all three sides and an angle opposite a known side.

We can use the cosine rule to connect the sides and angle in an equation:

$$a^2 = b^2 + c^2 - 2bc\cos A$$
$$21^2 = x^2 + (x + 9)^2 - 2x(x + 9)\cos 60°$$
$$441 = x^2 + x^2 + 9x + 9x + 81 - x(x + 9)$$
$$441 = 2x^2 + 18x + 81 - x^2 - 9x$$
$$441 = x^2 + 9x + 81$$
$$x^2 + 9x - 360 = 0$$
$$(x + 24)(x - 15) = 0$$

The cosine rule is identified by an "angle sandwich".
Substitute the values into the cosine rule equation.
Expand the brackets and simplify.
Set the quadratic equal to zero.
Factorise.
Only the positive solution is valid.

$$\cos 60° = \frac{1}{2}$$

x must be positive, therefore $x = 15$

Since x represented the distance from Hill A to Hill C the correct answer is 15 miles.

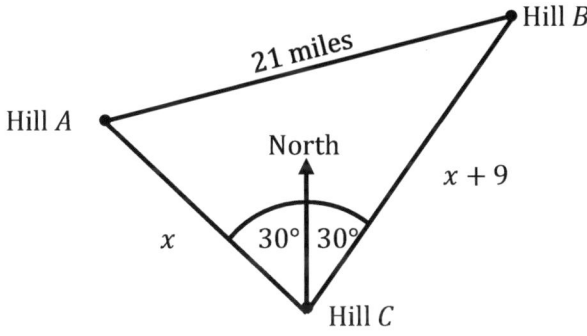

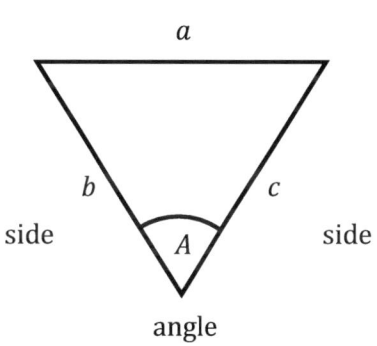

The angle sandwich indicating the cosine rule

8

We need to determine the frequency of the $20 < a \leq 50$ interval in 2012.
The frequency represented by each rectangle is equal to the area of the rectangle.
We do not know the frequency density scale so we will need to make up a scale and see how it relates to an expected total.

We do know that the area of the rectangles in each completed histogram will be 80 since this has not changed between the five years.
Notice that the oldest person was 54 in 2012 which means that five years later they would still be in the same $50 < a \leq 60$ interval.

We can start by letting the intervals on the frequency density scale increase by x units.
This allows us to form a table for the age distribution across the five years.
Since x is an unknown, we need to establish a link and an equation to solve.
This will be made clearer with a table:

Age interval	2012 frequency	2017 frequency
$0 < a \leq 20$	$20 \times 5.5x$	$20 \times 5.5x - 8$
$20 < a \leq 50$	Not given	$30 \times 8x$
$50 < a \leq 60$	$10 \times 8x$	$10 \times 8x + 2$

We know that there were eight fewer people in the $0 < a \leq 20$ interval so we subtract 8 from the 2012 value.
We know that there were two more people in the $50 < a \leq 60$ interval so we add 2 to the 2012 value.

We also know the 2017 column will sum to 80 which provides the equation link we were looking for:

$$20 \times 5.5x - 8 + 30 \times 8x + 10 \times 8x + 2 = 80 \quad \text{Set the 2017 frequency total to 80.}$$
$$110x - 8 + 240x + 80x + 2 = 80 \quad \text{Simplify the terms.}$$
$$430x - 6 = 80 \quad \text{Add 6.}$$
$$430x = 86 \quad \text{Divide by 430.}$$
$$x = 0.2$$

We now have the correct scale and can calculate the frequency of the $20 < a \leq 50$ interval in 2012.
$0 < a \leq 20$ had $20 \times 1.1 = 22$ people in 2012.
$50 < a \leq 60$ had $10 \times 1.6 = 16$ people in 2012.
The remaining people will be $80 - 22 - 16 = 42$.
The correct answer is 42.

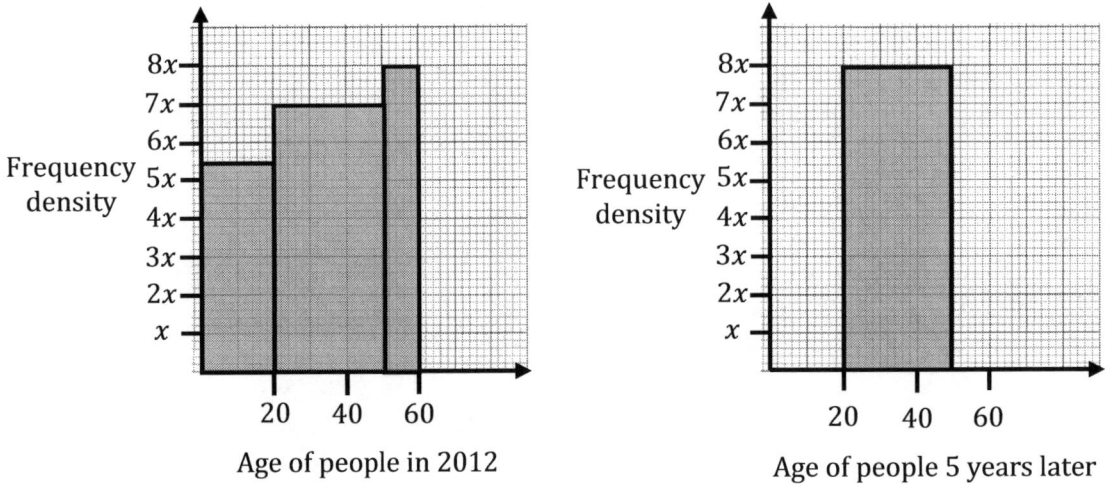

Age of people in 2012   Age of people 5 years later

9

This is a variation question involving delivery drivers, packages and time in hours.
These variables are connected by direct or inverse proportion.
This allows us to form some equations for x and y.
We begin by forming a table with headings delivery drivers, packages and time in hours.
Always input the start values which are given as "a delivery driver can deliver 10 packages in one hour".
The first condition given is that x delivery drivers can deliver y packages in four hours.
Make one change at a time to avoid confusion with the variables:

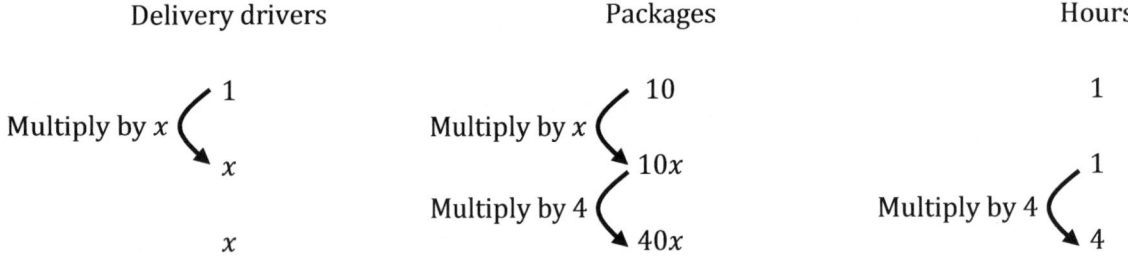

Drivers and packages are directly proportional so we multiply both by x.
Packages and hours are directly proportional so we multiply by 4.
We can see that x drivers deliver $40x$ packages in 4 hours.
However, we know that they deliver y packages so we have the first equation:
$y = 40x$ [1]

The second condition is that "if there are three more delivery drivers they can deliver 45 more packages in three and a half hours".

Now we input the second condition in the table, starting as before:

Delivery drivers	Packages	Hours

Multiply by $(x + 3)$ — 1 → $x + 3$

Multiply by $(x + 3)$ — 10 → $10(x + 3)$

Multiply by 3.5 — $x + 3$

Multiply by 3.5 — $35(x + 3)$

1

1

Multiply by 3.5 — 1 → 3.5

Drivers and packages are directly proportional so we multiply both by $(x + 3)$.
Packages and hours are directly proportional so we multiply by 3.5.
We can see that $(x + 3)$ drivers deliver $35(x + 3)$ packages in 3.5 hours.
However, we know that they deliver $y + 45$ packages so we have the second equation:

$$35(x + 3) = y + 45 \quad [2]$$

Substituting equation [1] in [2]:

$$35(x + 3) = 40x + 45 \qquad \text{Replace } y \text{ with } 40x.$$
$$35x + 105 = 40x + 45 \qquad \text{Expand the brackets.}$$
$$5x = 60 \qquad \text{Subtract } 35x \text{ and subtract } 45.$$
$$x = 12 \qquad \text{Divide by 5.}$$
$$y = 480 \qquad \text{Substitute } x = 12 \text{ into equation [1].}$$

The correct answers are $x = 12$ and $y = 480$.

10

This is a conditional probability with two events:

- Whether there has been a snowfall
- Whether the arctic fox finds food

We are given the probability of snowfall on a given day as 0.6.
The probability of no snowfall will be 0.4 as each branching must sum to 1.
We do not know any of the other branch probabilities so we will need to introduce our own variables.

Call the probability of finding food when there has been a snowfall x.
So the probability of not finding food when there has been a snowfall will be $1 - x$.

Call the probability of finding food when there has been no snowfall y.
So the probability of not finding food when there has been no snowfall will be $1 - y$.

We can represent this on a probability tree as shown below:

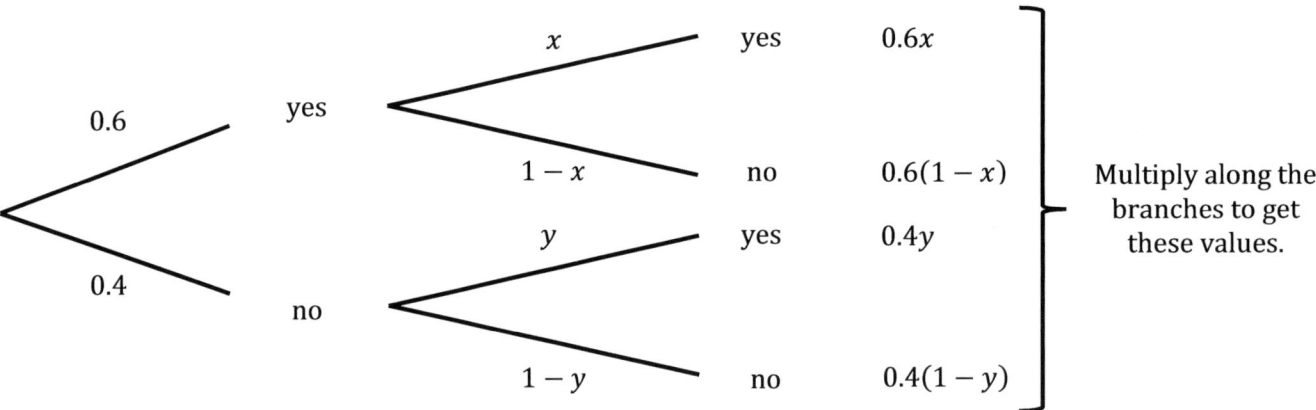

We can now form equations from the statements:

"The probability of the arctic fox finding food on a given day is $\frac{59}{150}$".

$$0.6x + 0.4y = \frac{59}{150} \quad [1]$$

"The probability of the arctic fox finding food when there has been a snowfall is 10% less than the probability of not finding food when there has been no snowfall".

$$0.6x = 0.9 \times 0.4(1 - y) \qquad \text{The multiplier for a 10\% decrease is 0.9.}$$
$$0.6x = 0.36(1 - y) \quad [2]$$

We can rearrange equation [1] to give:
$$0.6x = \frac{59}{150} - 0.4y$$

The left hand side of equation [1] is equal to [2] so now we can say the right hand sides are equal:

$$0.36(1 - y) = \frac{59}{150} - 0.4y$$
$$0.36 - 0.36y = \frac{59}{150} - 0.4y \qquad \text{Expand the brackets.}$$
$$54 - 54y = 59 - 60y \qquad \text{Multiply by 150.}$$
$$6y = 5 \qquad\qquad\qquad \text{Add } 60y.$$
$$y = \frac{5}{6} \qquad\qquad\qquad \text{Subtract 54.}$$
$$\text{Divide by 6.}$$

Substituting into equation [1]:
$$0.6x = \frac{59}{150} - 0.4y$$
$$= \frac{59}{150} - 0.4 \times \frac{5}{6}$$
$$= 0.06$$

We were asked "find the probability of the arctic fox finding food after a snowfall".
This was represented by $0.6x$ which we have found to be 0.06.

Exercise 3

1

The triangle ABC is shown.
Point P lies on BC such that the ratio $BC : BP = 5 : 2$
What is the ratio of the areas of triangles $ACP : ABP$?

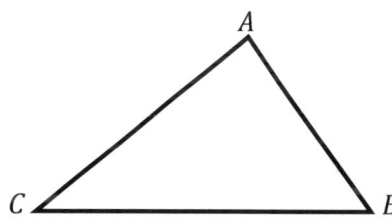

2

$PQRS$ is a trapezium with PQ parallel to SR.
M is the midpoint of the line PS.
N is the midpoint of the line QR.
The length $PQ = x$
The length $SR = y$

Prove algebraically that the length $MN = \dfrac{x+y}{2}$

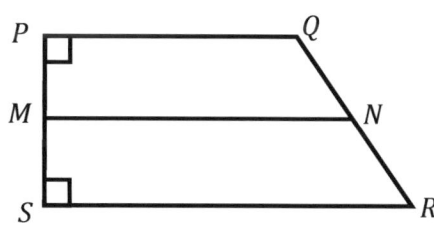

3

The diagram shows a trapezium $ABCD$.
E is a point on AB.
F is a point on DC.
$AD = a, EF = x$ and $BC = b$ and they are all parallel.
The trapezium is to be split into two trapeziums along the line EF.
$DF = c$ and $FC = d$
$c : d = 2 : 1$
Trapezium $ADFE$ and $BCFE$ have the same area.
Find the value of x in terms of a and b.

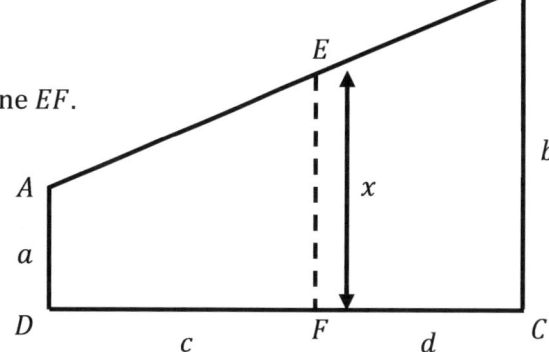

4

n is an integer.

For which value of k will $n^2 + 6n + k$ always be a square number?

5 calculator

The diagram shows a trapezium $ABCD$.

$AB = 39$cm

$BC = 12$cm

$DC = 52$cm

$AD = 5$cm

Calculate the area of the trapezium $ABCD$.

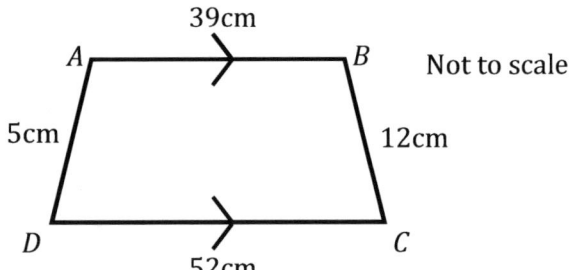

6

Factorise $4x^2 - 9(y-2)^2$

7

A solid cylinder has radius r and height h.

The volume of the cylinder is V.

The total surface area of the cylinder is A.

If $h = 4$cm, what value of r would make the ratio $V : A = 1 : 1$?

8

Polygon A has a sides.

Polygon B has $3a$ sides.

Both polygons are regular.

The exterior angle of polygon A is 6° greater than the exterior angle of a polygon B.

Find the value of a.

9

The right-angled triangle PQR is shown.

Angle PQR is a right angle.

S is a point on RP.

$SP = SQ$

Find the ratio of $SP : RP$

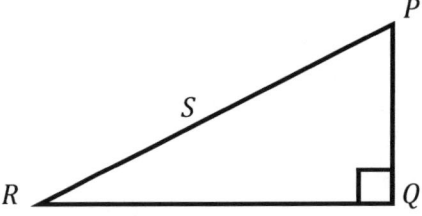

10

A triangle has sides of length $p^2 + q^2$, $2pq$ and $p^2 - q^2$ where p and q are integers with $p > q$.

Prove that the triangle is right-angled.

Exercise 3 Solutions

1

When calculating the area of two triangles that have the same height, the factor determining their area is the base length.

The perpendicular distance from the side BC to the point A is the height for triangles ACP and ABP.

The base length ratio $CP : PB = 3 : 2$

This means the areas of the triangles $ACP : ABP$ will have the ratio $3 : 2$

See the diagram below.

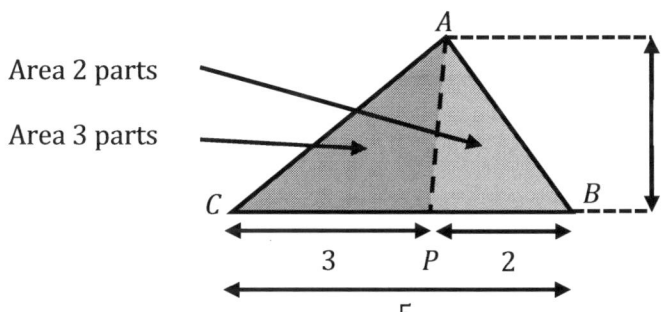

Area 2 parts

Area 3 parts

Common height h

The base ratio divides the area ratio when the triangles share a common height.

We can prove this fact algebraically.

Let the height be h, the length $CP = 3x$ and the length $PB = 2x$.

$$\text{area of triangle } ACP = \frac{1}{2}bh$$
$$= \frac{1}{2} \times 3x \times h$$
$$= \frac{3}{2}xh$$
$$\text{area of triangle } ABP = \frac{1}{2}bh$$
$$= \frac{1}{2} \times 2x \times h$$
$$= xh$$

Ratio of areas,

$$\text{area of triangle } ACP : \text{area of triangle } ABP = \frac{3}{2}xh : xh$$
$$= \frac{3}{2} : 1 \qquad \text{Divide by } xh.$$
$$= 3 : 2 \qquad \text{Multiply by 2.}$$

Remember you can multiply and divide ratios as you would an equation.

2

We can extend a vertical line from R which meets a projection of the line PQ.

Call this intersection point T.

We can also extend the line MN so that it intersects the vertical line RT at a point we can call V.

The triangles QRT and NRV are similar because all three of their angles are equal.

Since the point N is the midpoint of QR the lengths of the triangle NRV will all be half those of triangle QRT.

The side PS is perpendicular to the side PQ.

This means that PQ and SR are parallel sides, which they would be in a trapezium.

We can say that the length $QT = y - x$

Since we know that NV will be half this length we can say $NV = \frac{y-x}{2}$

We can now form an expression for the length MN:

$$MN = MV - NV$$
$$= y - \frac{y-x}{2}$$
$$= y - \frac{y}{2} + \frac{x}{2}$$
$$= \frac{y}{2} + \frac{x}{2}$$
$$= \frac{y+x}{2}$$

Substitute for MV and NV in terms of x and y.

Split the fraction into two fractions with the same denominator:

$$\frac{y-x}{2} = \frac{y}{2} - \frac{x}{2}$$

Remember that you are subtracting $\left(\frac{y}{2} - \frac{x}{2}\right)$.

Simplify and combine to form a fraction with common denominator 2.

This completes the proof.

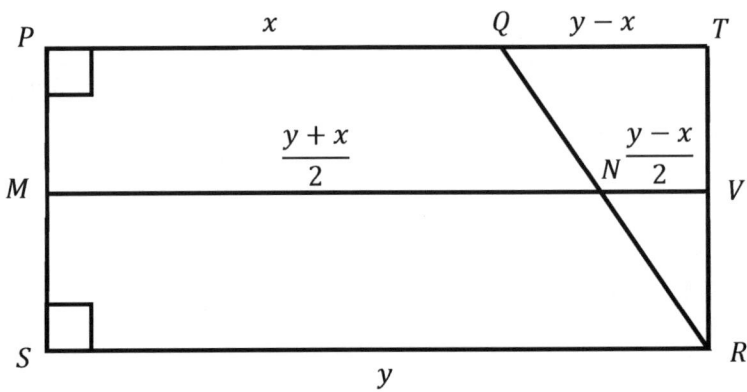

3

The general formula for the area of a trapezium is:

$$\text{area} = \frac{1}{2}h(a+b)$$

a and b are the parallel sides and h the perpendicular distance between them.

We know the areas of trapezium $ADFE$ and $BCFE$ are the same and this forms the basis of an equation.

We know the ratio $c : d = 2 : 1$ so we can say that $c = 2d$.

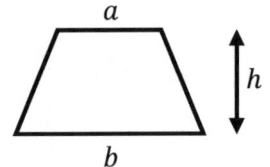

Cross multiplying a ratio

$$2 : 1$$
$$c : d$$
$$c = 2d$$

$$\text{area } ADFE = \text{area } BCFE$$
$$\frac{1}{2}c(a+x) = \frac{1}{2}d(x+b)$$
$$\frac{1}{2}(2d)(a+x) = \frac{1}{2}d(x+b)$$
$$d(a+x) = \frac{1}{2}d(x+b)$$
$$2(a+x) = x+b$$
$$2a + 2x = x+b$$
$$2a + x = b$$
$$x = b - 2a$$

Replace c with $2d$.
Simplify: $\frac{1}{2}(2d) = d$

Cancel d from both sides.
Multiply by 2.
Expand the brackets.
Subtract x.
Subtract $2a$

The correct answer is $x = b - 2a$.

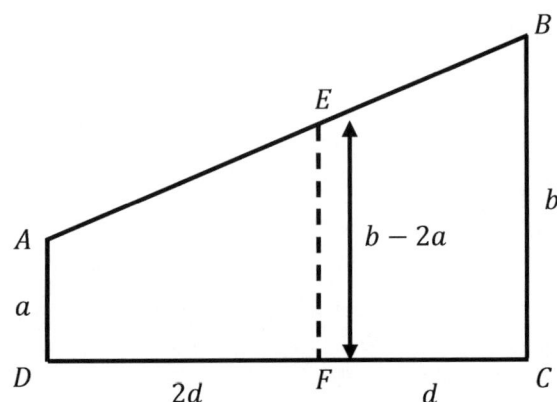

4

We can start by defining a square number:
A square number is the square of an integer, e.g. 25 is the square of 5.
This definition is not restricted to just numbers; it can involve expressions, too, e.g. a^2 or $(a + 2)^2$
This is true if the value of a is an integer.
We need to get the expression $n^2 + 6n + k$ into a form that would be written as $(some\ expression)^2$
We can see that the expression is in the form of a quadratic.
We may be able to complete the square to get the required form.
Remember completing the square for a quadratic of the form $x^2 + ax + b$:

$$x^2 + ax + b \equiv \left(x + \frac{a}{2}\right)^2 + b - \frac{a^2}{4}$$

The symbol $\equiv$ means identical to; we are not dealing with an equation here, just rearranging the terms so that they are identical.
For the given expression we obtain:

$$n^2 + 6n + k \equiv (n + 3)^2 + k - 9$$

We can see that the term $(n + 3)^2$ on its own must be square since n is an integer but the $k - 9$ part currently prevents the whole expression being square.
However, if $k = 9$ we are left with $(n + 3)^2$ which is the required form.
The correct answer is $k = 9$.

5

We know the general formula for the area of a trapezium is:

$$\text{area} = \frac{1}{2}h(a + b)$$

a and b are the parallel sides and h the perpendicular distance between them.
The problem here is that we do not have the perpendicular height.
Since we know the non-parallel sides AD and BC, there is another way of finding the area without the need for the perpendicular height.
The sides AD and BC can be extended until they meet, we will say at point E.

We can then say that triangles EAB and EDC are similar because they have identical angles:
Angle AEB is shared.
Angle EAB is equal to angle EDC because they are corresponding angles.
Angle EBA is equal to angle ECD because they are corresponding angles.

Now we need the area of triangles EAB and EDC.
The difference in area of the triangles is the trapezium area.
Notice the ratio of the side lengths $AB : DC = 39 : 52$
This simplifies to $3 : 4$
We know that this ratio will be the same for $EA : ED$ and $EB : EC$ because of similar triangles.
You can think of AD or BC making up one part of the four parts in the ratio.
This means that $EA = 15$cm and $EB = 36$cm.

We now have all three sides of the triangles (see diagrams below).
If we find an angle between two of the sides we can then use the sine area formula to find the triangle area.

To find the angle we need the cosine rule which we will apply to triangle EAB:

$$a^2 = b^2 + c^2 - 2bc\cos A$$
$$39^2 = 15^2 + 36^2 - 2 \times 15 \times 36\cos A$$
$$39^2 - 15^2 - 36^2 = -1080\cos A$$
$$\cos A = \frac{39^2 - 15^2 - 36^2}{-1080}$$
$$= 0$$
$$A = \cos^{-1} 0$$
$$= 90°$$

The angle sandwich of the cosine rule

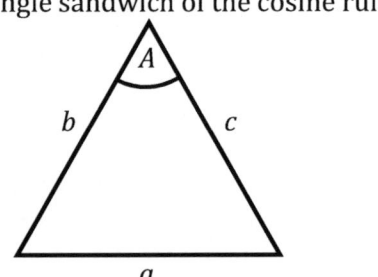

Notice that the two triangles are right angled.
This means the area can be found using $\frac{1}{2}bh$ instead of the sine area formula:

area of triangle $EDC = \dfrac{1}{2} \times 20 \times 48$
$$= 480$$
area of triangle $EAB = \dfrac{1}{2} \times 15 \times 36$
$$= 270$$

The difference in area is the trapezium area:
area of trapezium $ABCD = 480 - 270$
$$= 210$$
The correct answer is 210cm^2.

The diagram on the left is a sketch of the given problem.
The diagram on the right is a more accurate representation of the problem.

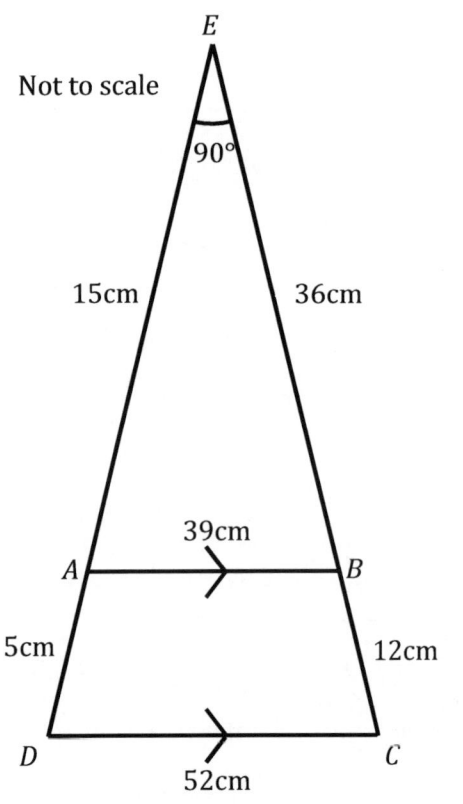

More accurate diagram

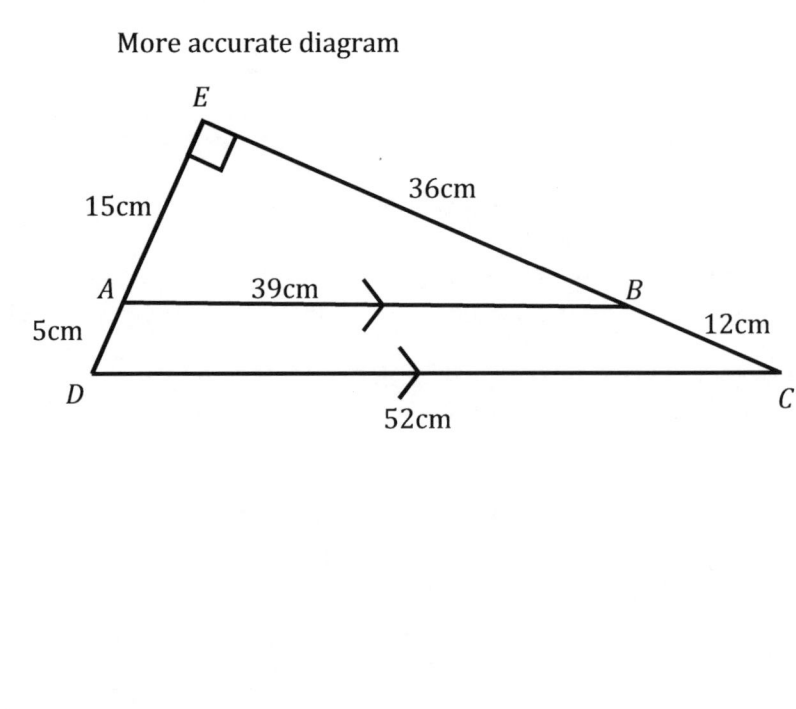

6

This expression is the form of the difference of two squares: $a^2 - b^2 \equiv (a+b)(a-b)$.

Remember to square root each term of the expression: $4x^2 = (2x)^2$ and $9(y-2)^2 = \left(3(y-2)\right)^2$

$$4x^2 - 9(y-2)^2 \equiv \left(2x + 3(y-2)\right)\left(2x - 3(y-2)\right)$$
$$\equiv (2x + 3y - 6)(2x - 3y + 6)$$

The correct answer is $(2x + 3y - 6)(2x - 3y + 6)$.

7

We need to find the radius such that the numeric values of the area and volume of the cylinder are equal.
Then the ratio $V : A = 1 : 1$

The volume of a cylinder is given by:

volume $= \pi r^2 h$

$\qquad = \pi r^2 \times 4 \qquad\qquad h = 4$

$\qquad = 4\pi r^2$

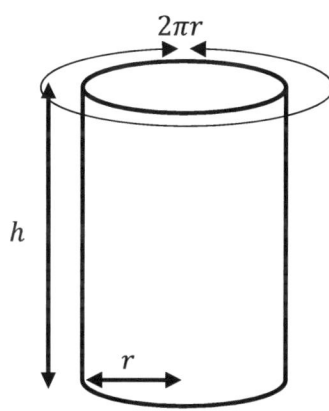

The surface area of a solid cylinder is formed from:

area $= 2 \times$ end circle areas $+$ curved rectangle between the circles

$\qquad = 2 \times \pi r^2 + 2\pi rh$

$\qquad = 2\pi r^2 + 8\pi r \qquad\qquad h = 4$

We now set the volume and area equal to each other and solve for r.

volume $=$ area

$\qquad 4\pi r^2 = 2\pi r^2 + 8\pi r$

$\qquad\quad 2r = r + 4 \qquad\qquad$ Divide by $2\pi r$.

$\qquad\quad\ r = 4 \qquad\qquad\quad$ Subtract r.

The correct answer is $r = 4$cm.

8

The sum of the exterior angles in a regular polygon is 360°.
To find the size of one exterior angle we divide 360 by the number of sides.
We know that when this calculation is performed for polygon A and B the difference in angle size is 6°.
We use this to form and solve an equation for a:

exterior angle of polygon $A = $ exterior angle of polygon $B + 6$

$$\frac{360}{a} = \frac{360}{3a} + 6$$

$$\frac{360}{a} = \frac{120}{a} + 6 \qquad\qquad \frac{360}{3a} = \frac{120}{a}$$

$$360 = 120 + 6a \qquad\qquad \text{Multiply by } a.$$

$6a = 240 \qquad\qquad\qquad\qquad\qquad$ Subtract 120.

$\ a = 40 \qquad\qquad\qquad\qquad\qquad$ Divide by 6.

This means polygon A had 40 sides and polygon B had 120 sides.

9

We can begin labelling the diagram shown below.

To find the ratio we need to determine the relative sizes of the sides SP and RP.

$SP = SQ$ so the triangle SPQ is isosceles.

Let angle $SPQ = x$.

Then angle $SQP = x$ because triangle SPQ is isosceles.

Angle $PSQ = 180 - 2x$

Angle $RSQ = 180 - (180 - 2x)$ 180 degrees on a straight line.

$\qquad\quad = 180 - 180 + 2x$

$\qquad\quad = 2x$

Angle $RQS = 90 - x$

Angle $SRQ = 180 - (90 - x) - 2x$ 180 degrees in a triangle.

$\qquad\quad = 180 - 90 + x - 2x$

$\qquad\quad = 90 - x$

Notice that the angles SRQ and RQS are equal.

This means triangle RQS is isosceles and that sides RS and SQ are equal.

Since $SP = SQ$ we can say that $RS = SP$.

This means the ratio $SP : RP = 1 : 2$

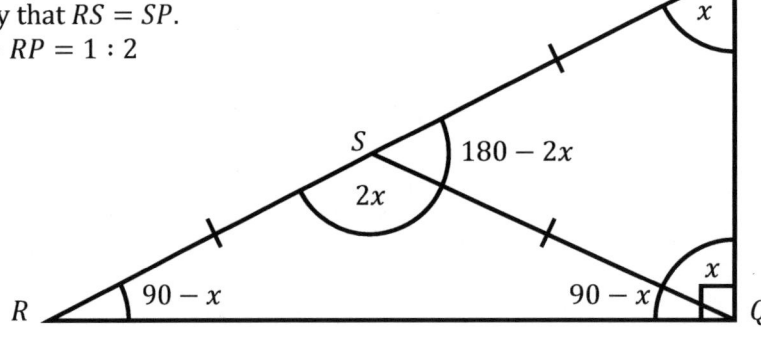

10

If a triangle is right-angled then its sides must relate by Pythagoras: $a^2 + b^2 = c^2$

The sum of the squares of two of these sides must equal the square of the third side.

We begin by squaring each term:

First side

$(p^2 + q^2)^2 = (p^2 + q^2)(p^2 + q^2)$

$\qquad\qquad = p^4 + p^2q^2 + p^2q^2 + q^4$

$\qquad\qquad = p^4 + 2p^2q^2 + q^4$

Second side

$(2pq)^2 = 4p^2q^2$

Third side

$(p^2 - q^2)^2 = (p^2 - q^2)(p^2 - q^2)$

$\qquad\qquad = p^4 - p^2q^2 - p^2q^2 + q^4$

$\qquad\qquad = p^4 - 2p^2q^2 + q^4$

We can see that the sum of the second and third side squares is equal to the first side square:

$4p^2q^2 + p^4 - 2p^2q^2 + q^4 = p^4 + 2p^2q^2 + q^4$

This proves that the triangle is right-angled.

Exercise 4

1

$$\frac{x - y}{x + y} = \frac{4}{5}$$

Find the value of $\dfrac{3x}{4y}$

2

The frequency tree shows information about a survey of pet ownership at a local veterinary practice. Owners were asked if they owned a dog or cat and whether their pet was above or below 7 years of age. There were 60 cats in the survey.

The ratios,
7 years or above cats : 7 years or above dogs = 2 : 3
under 7 years cats : under 7 years dogs = 2 : 3

The probability of selecting a pet that is 7 years or above given that the pet is a dog is $\dfrac{3}{5}$.

Complete the frequency tree.

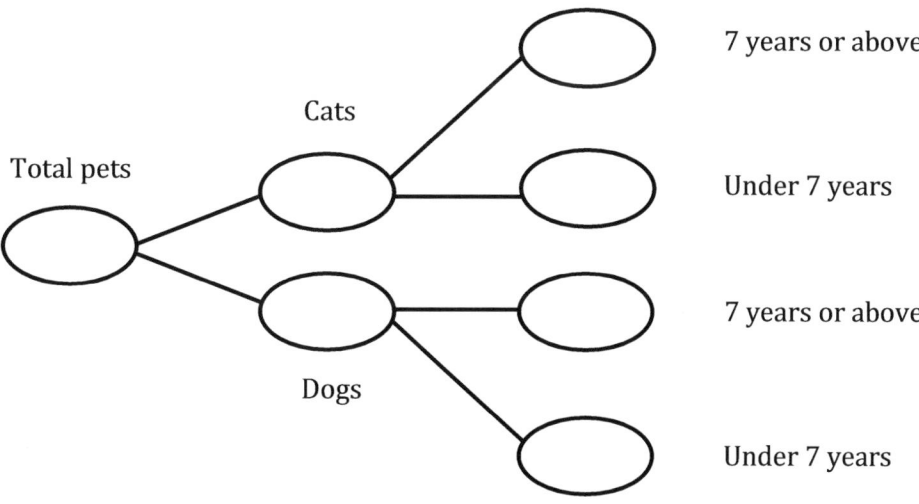

3 calculator

Triangle ABC is shown.
CBD is a straight line.
$\vec{AC} = \mathbf{a}$ and $\vec{CB} = \mathbf{b}$

The lines $DB : BC = c : d$
The lines $AE : EC = 2 : 3$
The lines $AF : FB = 9 : 8$

EFD is a straight line.
Find $c : d$ in its simplest form.

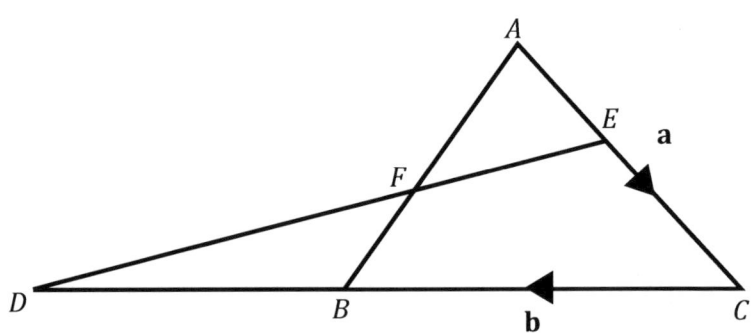

4

In the Venn diagram

ξ = number of customers sampled from a bank.
C = number of people with current accounts
S = number of people with savings accounts

There are 300 people in the sample.
The probability of selecting a customer with a savings account given they have a current account is $\frac{3}{8}$.

The probability of selecting a customer with a current account given they have a savings account is $\frac{25}{43}$.

46 people have neither a savings nor a current account.
How many people have a current account only?

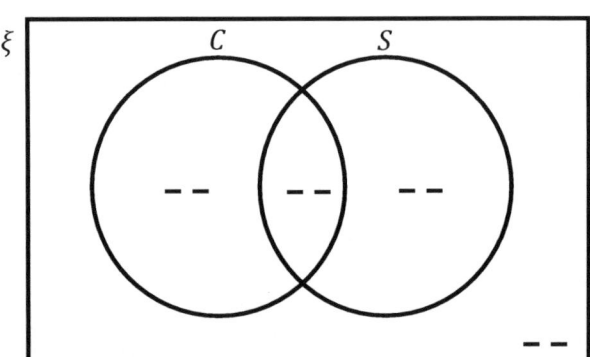

5

The shape shown is formed from two large sectors and two squares with sectors removed.
The large sectors have radius $2r$ and the small sectors have radius r.
The shaded area is equal to $(288 + 54\pi)\text{cm}^2$.
Find the value of r.

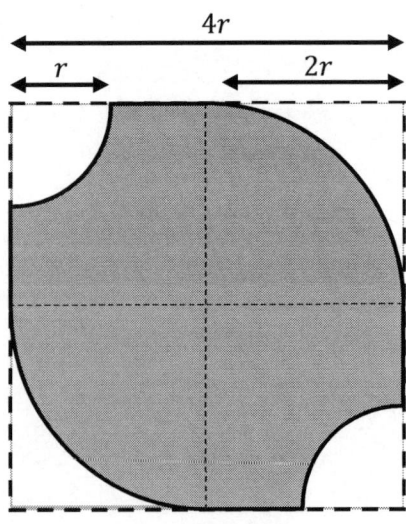

6

The graph shows the curve with equation $y = bx^2 + cx + d$ and the line with equation $y = 10x$.
The curve intersects the x-axis at the points $(a, 0)$ and $(3a, 0)$.
The curve intersects the y-axis at the point $(0, 6a^2)$
The line intersects the curve at the point $(6a, 60a)$.
Find the value of a.

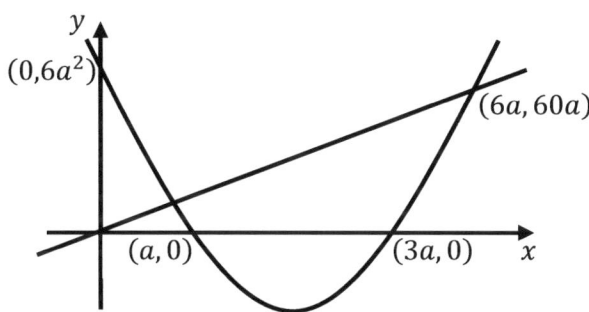

7 calculator

There are 30 counters in a bag.
The counters are red, green and blue.
Two counters are selected and not replaced.
The probability of selecting a red and blue in either order is $\frac{16}{87}$
The probability of selecting two reds is $\frac{28}{435}$
What is the probability of selecting two green counters?

8 calculator

There are red, blue and yellow beads in a box.
Two beads are selected and not replaced.
The probability of selecting two red beads is $\frac{2}{51}$
Six more beads, none of them red, are added to the box.
The probability of selecting two red beads now is $\frac{1}{46}$
How many beads were originally in the box?

9

A teacher makes predictions about whether his students will pass or fail an exam.
The probability of passing given that a pass was predicted is 0.9.
The probability of failing given that fail was predicted is 0.7.
The probability of passing is 0.78.
Find the probability of the teacher predicting a pass.

10 calculator

Two boxes contain red and blue balls.
Box A contains five red and seven blue balls.
Box B contains four red and nine blue balls.
A ball is transferred from Box A to Box B and then a ball is selected from Box B.
Find the probability that the ball transferred is blue given that the ball selected is blue.

Exercise 4 Solutions

1

It is not clear with this algebra problem exactly how we will get to $\frac{3x}{4y}$ from $\frac{x-y}{x+y} = \frac{4}{5}$.

After some operations on the start equation it may become clearer as to where the result comes from:

$\dfrac{x-y}{x+y} = \dfrac{4}{5}$ Multiply by 5.

$\dfrac{5(x-y)}{x+y} = 4$ Multiply by $(x+y)$.

$5(x-y) = 4(x+y)$ Expand the brackets

$5x - 5y = 4x + 4y$ Subtract $4x$.

$x = 9y$ Add $5y$.

$\dfrac{x}{y} = 9$ Divide by y.

    Now we have a multiple of the required answer.

$\dfrac{3}{4} \times \dfrac{x}{y} = \dfrac{3}{4} \times 9$ Multiply by $\frac{3}{4}$ to get the required result.

$\dfrac{3x}{4y} = \dfrac{27}{4}$

The correct answer is $\frac{27}{4}$.

2

For this frequency tree question, several of the missing values are given as ratios.
We can multiply each ratio by a factor that would represent the original values.
For the first ratio,

7 years or above cats : 7 years or above dogs $= 2 : 3$
$$= 2x : 3x$$

x is a multiplier that gives the original values.

For the second ratio,
under 7 years cats : under 7 years dogs $= 2 : 3$
$$= 2y : 3y$$

y is a multiplier that gives the original values.
We know there were 60 cats.
These can be added to the frequency tree.

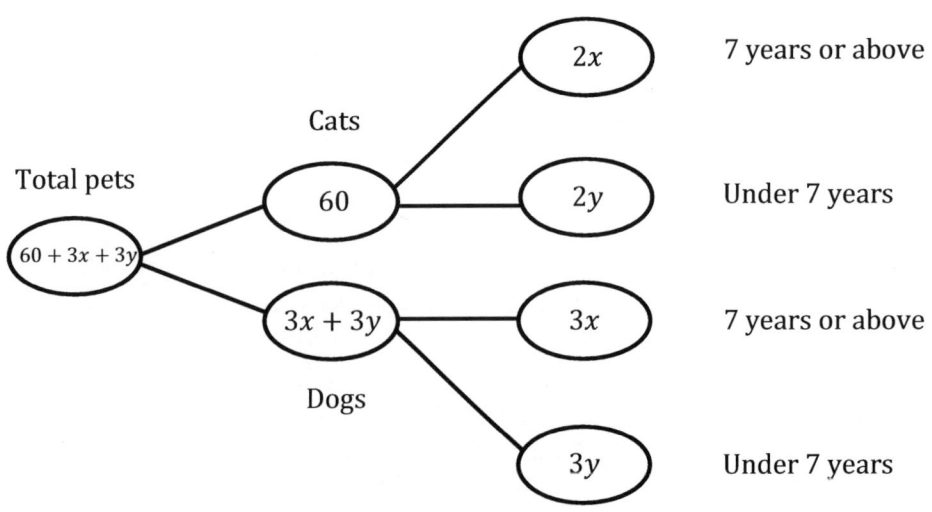

We can now form some equations from the other information given.
We can say $2x + 2y = 60$ or $x + y = 30$ [1]
We can say that $60 + 3x + 3y$ represents the total pets.
We know that the probability of selecting a pet that is 7 years or above given that the pet is a dog is $\frac{3}{5}$.
From this we can say:

$$\frac{\text{number of dogs 7 years and above}}{\text{total number of dogs}} = \frac{3}{5}$$

$$\frac{3x}{3x + 3y} = \frac{3}{5} \qquad \text{Cancel the factor of 3 on the left hand side.}$$

$$\frac{x}{x + y} = \frac{3}{5} \quad [2]$$

We have two equations to solve for x and y.
Substituting equation [1] into [2]:

$$\frac{x}{30} = \frac{3}{5} \qquad \qquad \text{Replace } x + y \text{ with 30.}$$

$$x = \frac{90}{5} \qquad \qquad \text{Multiply by 30.}$$

$$= 18 \qquad \qquad \text{Simplify.}$$

$$y = 30 - 18 \qquad \qquad y = 30 - x \text{ from equation [1]}.$$

$$= 12$$

Now we can complete the frequency tree as shown.

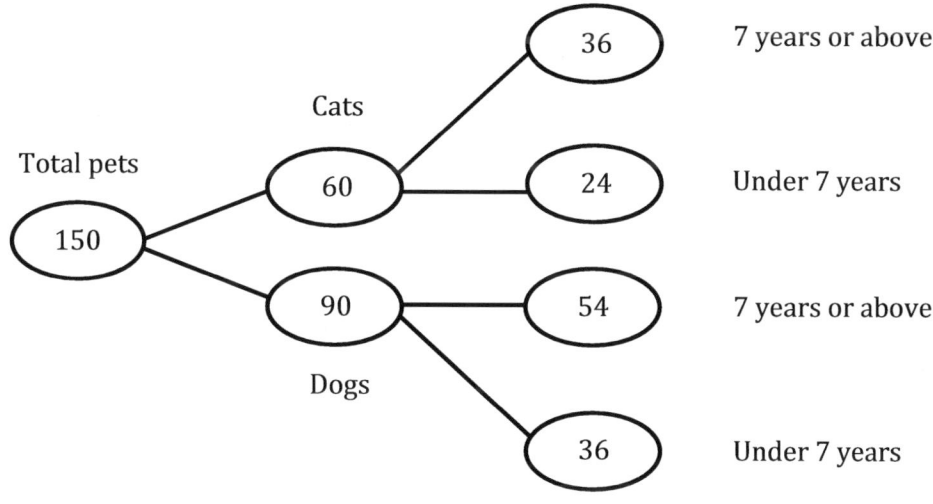

3

If EFD is a straight line then the vector $\overrightarrow{ED}$ must be a scalar multiple of the vector $\overrightarrow{EF}$.
This means the vectors are parallel and start from the same point which implies they are on the same straight line.
We write this as $\overrightarrow{ED} = k\overrightarrow{EF}$ where k is a scalar multiple to be determined.
With vector problems, you can only define vectors in terms of vectors you know, in this case $\mathbf{a}$ and $\mathbf{b}$.
The vectors required will be determined by the route taken to get from point to point.
$\overrightarrow{ED} = \overrightarrow{EC} + \overrightarrow{CD}$ and $\overrightarrow{EF} = \overrightarrow{EA} + \overrightarrow{AF}$ so we need the vectors $\overrightarrow{EC}, \overrightarrow{CD}, \overrightarrow{EA}$ and $\overrightarrow{AF}$.
We need to add some more vectors to the diagram using the ratios provided.

$AE : EC = 2 : 3$ which means $\overrightarrow{AE} = \frac{2}{5}\mathbf{a}$ (or $\overrightarrow{EA} = -\frac{2}{5}\mathbf{a}$) and $\overrightarrow{EC} = \frac{3}{5}\mathbf{a}$.

We also need to find the vector for $\overrightarrow{AF}$.

$AF : FB = 9 : 8$ which means $\overrightarrow{AF} = \frac{9}{17}\overrightarrow{AB}$

$$\overrightarrow{AF} = \frac{9}{17}\overrightarrow{AB}$$
$$= \frac{9}{17}\left(\overrightarrow{AC} + \overrightarrow{CB}\right)$$
$$= \frac{9}{17}(\mathbf{a} + \mathbf{b})$$

We can now find the vector $\overrightarrow{EF}$:

$$\overrightarrow{EF} = \overrightarrow{EA} + \overrightarrow{AF}$$
$$= -\frac{2}{5}\mathbf{a} + \frac{9}{17}(\mathbf{a} + \mathbf{b})$$
$$= -\frac{2}{5}\mathbf{a} + \frac{9}{17}\mathbf{a} + \frac{9}{17}\mathbf{b}$$
$$= \frac{11}{85}\mathbf{a} + \frac{9}{17}\mathbf{b}$$

We know that $\overrightarrow{ED} = k\overrightarrow{EF}$.

If a vector is defined in terms of two components, namely $\mathbf{a}$ and $\mathbf{b}$, then any scalar multiple will apply to the coefficients of both $\mathbf{a}$ and $\mathbf{b}$.

For example, consider a vector $\mathbf{a} + \mathbf{b}$.

A parallel vector would be $2\mathbf{a} + 2\mathbf{b}$.

Both coefficients were multiplied by scale factor 2 to make the vector parallel.

By coefficient we mean the number in front of a letter, so $3x$ has a coefficient of 3.

We can find a scale factor if we can find the coefficient of either $\mathbf{a}$ or $\mathbf{b}$.

In the vector $\overrightarrow{ED}$,

$$\overrightarrow{ED} = \overrightarrow{EC} + \overrightarrow{CD}$$
$$= \frac{3}{5}\mathbf{a} + \overrightarrow{CD} \qquad \overrightarrow{CD} \text{ is in terms of } \mathbf{b} \text{ only.}$$

We know the coefficients of $\mathbf{a}$ for both $\overrightarrow{ED}$ and $\overrightarrow{EF}$.

We can now find the scale factor k by division:

$$\frac{3}{5} \div \frac{11}{85} = \frac{51}{11}$$

So $k = \frac{51}{11}$.

The scalar multiple k is $\frac{51}{11}$.

$$\frac{11}{85}\mathbf{a} + \frac{9}{17}\mathbf{b}$$

$$\times \frac{51}{11} \downarrow \qquad \downarrow \times \frac{51}{11}$$

$$\frac{3}{5}\mathbf{a} + \frac{27}{11}\mathbf{b}$$

Now we multiply the $\mathbf{b}$ coefficient in $\overrightarrow{EF}$ by this scale factor:

$$\frac{9}{17} \times \frac{51}{11} = \frac{27}{11}$$

The vector $\overrightarrow{CD}$ is given by $\frac{27}{11}\mathbf{b}$.

$\overrightarrow{CB} = \mathbf{b}$ which is the same as $\frac{11}{11}\mathbf{b}$.

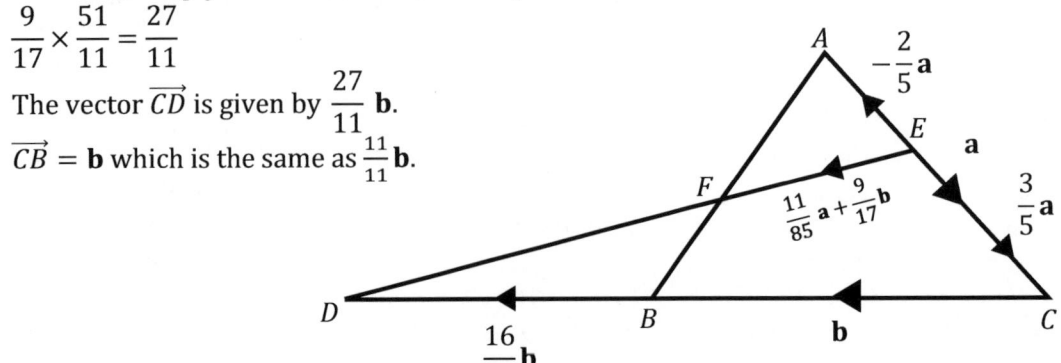

We can now find $\overrightarrow{BD}$:

$$\overrightarrow{BD} = \overrightarrow{BC} + \overrightarrow{CD}$$
$$= -\frac{11}{11}\mathbf{b} + \frac{27}{11}\mathbf{b}$$
$$= \frac{16}{11}\mathbf{b}$$

The required ratio is $DB : BC = 16 : 11$ which is the same as $c : d = 16 : 11$.

4

We are given the total of all the customers as 300 and the number of customers who have neither a current account nor a savings account as 46.

This means the customers who had a current or savings account will be $300 - 46 = 254$.

The two probabilities given are conditional.

They can also be converted to ratios for the unknown values in the Venn diagram.

The probability of selecting a customer with a savings account given they have a current account is $\frac{3}{8}$.

This means that of the 8 parts representing a current account, 3 parts represent the customers with both current and savings accounts.

This means 5 parts have current accounts only.

The probability of selecting a customer with a current account given they have a savings account is $\frac{25}{43}$.

This means that of the 43 parts representing a savings account, 25 parts represent the customers with both current and savings accounts.

This means 18 parts have savings accounts only.

Notice that we have two ratios representing three variables with one variable common to both ratios.

If we call the three unknown values a, b and c as shown in the diagram, we can write the following ratios:

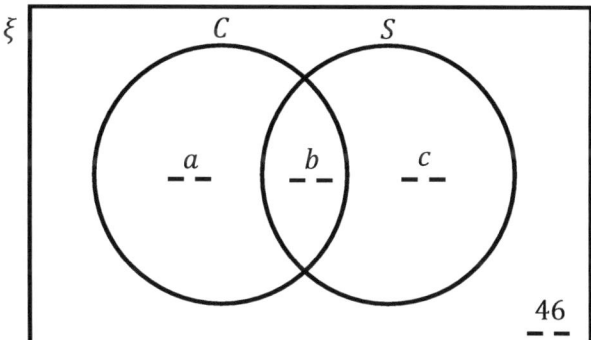

$$a : b = 5 : 3$$

$$b : c = 25 : 18$$

When two ratios share a common variable (in this case b) we can combine them into one ratio for all three variables using common multiples.

Notice that b is represented by 3 and 25 in each ratio.

The lowest common multiple of 3 and 25 is 75.

If we multiply the first ratio by 25 and the second ratio by 3 we will have a common multiple in both.

$5 : 3 = 125 : 75$

$25 : 18 = 75 : 54$

This allows us to combine into one ratio:

$a : b : c = 125 : 75 : 54$

We know that $a + b + c = 254$

The ratio as it stands already sums to this value: $125 + 75 + 54 = 254$

This means these values are the actual values.

The number of customers with a current account only will be 125.

5

We can split the shape into four:

- two identical sectors of radius $2r$ (which together form a semicircle)
- two identical squares each with identical sectors of radius r removed (which together form a semicircle).

We are given the area of the shape so we can form an equation:

Before the algebra, a visual representation can be helpful.

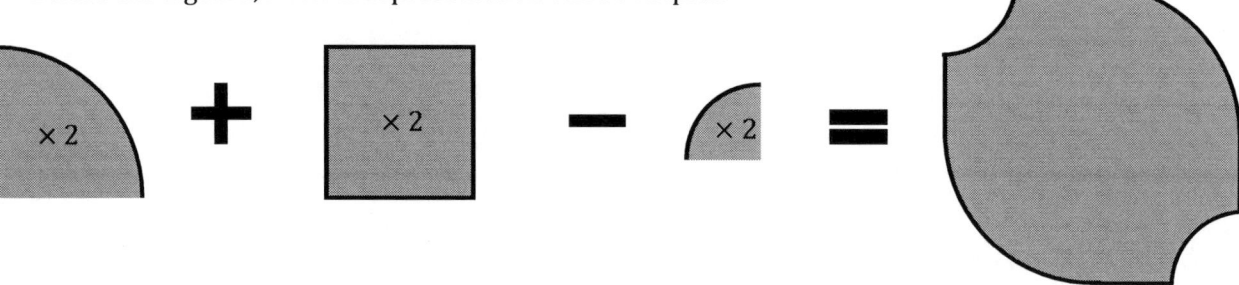

$2 \times$ large sector area $+ 2 \times$ square area $- 2 \times$ small sector area $= 288 + 54\pi$

$$2 \times \frac{\pi(2r)^2}{4} + 2 \times (2r)^2 - 2 \times \frac{\pi r^2}{4} = 288 + 54\pi$$

$$2\pi r^2 + 8r^2 - \frac{\pi r^2}{2} = 288 + 54\pi \qquad \text{Expand the brackets.}$$

$$\frac{3}{2}\pi r^2 + 8r^2 = 288 + 54\pi \qquad \text{Collect the } \pi r^2 \text{ terms.}$$

$$r^2 \left(\frac{3}{2}\pi + 8\right) = 288 + 54\pi \qquad \text{Factorise the } r^2.$$

$$r^2 = \frac{288 + 54\pi}{\frac{3}{2}\pi + 8} \qquad \text{Divide by } \frac{3}{2}\pi + 8.$$

$$= \frac{576 + 108\pi}{3\pi + 16} \qquad \text{Multiply all terms in the fraction by 2.}$$

$$= \frac{36(16 + 3\pi)}{3\pi + 16} \qquad \text{Factorise the numerator.}$$

$$= 36 \qquad \text{Cancel } 3\pi + 16.$$

$$r = 6 \qquad \text{Square root.}$$

The correct answer is $r = 6$cm.

6

We can use the y-intercept to find the value of d, this is when $x = 0$.

$y = bx^2 + cx + d$

$6a^2 = b(0)^2 + c(0) + d$

$d = 6a^2$

We now look at the roots given as a and $3a$.

They tell us what the quadratic simplifies down to after factorising.

On their own though, they do not tell us the complete quadratic equation required.

For example,

If we factorise and solve $x^2 + 5x + 6 = 0$ we obtain $(x + 2)(x + 3) = 0$

So we conclude that the roots (or solutions) are $x = -2$ and $x = -3$.

But if we factorise and solve $2x^2 + 10x + 12 = 0$ we obtain $2(x + 2)(x + 3) = 0$

This again gives the solutions as $x = -2$ and $x = -3$ but they both came from different quadratic equations.

Notice that the second quadratic $2x^2 + 10x + 12 = 0$ was twice the quadratic $x^2 + 5x + 6 = 0$.

Each term was multiplied by 2.

This multiplier is the coefficient of the x^2 term and that is what we need to find for the quadratic:
$y = bx^2 + cx + d$
We can say that our quadratic will be of the form $n(x - a)(x - 3a)$ where n is the multiplier in question.
Remember to swap the signs of the roots when you factorise after inspecting a graph.

If we multiply out $n(x - a)(x - 3a)$ we obtain:
$$n(x - a)(x - 3a) = n(x^2 - 3ax - ax + 3a^2)$$
$$= nx^2 - 4nax + 3na^2$$

The term $3na^2$ represents the y-intercept, which we already know to be $6a^2$.
Since $3na^2 \equiv 6a^2$ (they are identical) we conclude that n must be 2.
Substituting $n = 2$ back into the quadratic $nx^2 - 4nax + 3na^2$ we obtain $2x^2 - 8ax + 6a^2$.
We are now in a position to determine the value of a.
We are told that the curve intercepts the line $y = 10x$ at the point $(6a, 60a)$.
We can substitute these coordinates into the equation $y = 2x^2 - 8ax + 6a^2$ to find a.

$60a = 2(6a)^2 - 8a(6a) + 6a^2$ Substitute $x = 6a$ and $y = 60a$ into the equation.
$\quad\;\, = 72a^2 - 48a^2 + 6a^2$ Simplify.
$\quad\;\, = 30a^2$
$30a = 60$ Divide by a (because we know it is never zero from the graph).
$\quad a = 2$ Divide by 30.
The correct answer is $a = 2$.

The quadratic curve has the equation $y = 2x^2 - 16x + 24$.

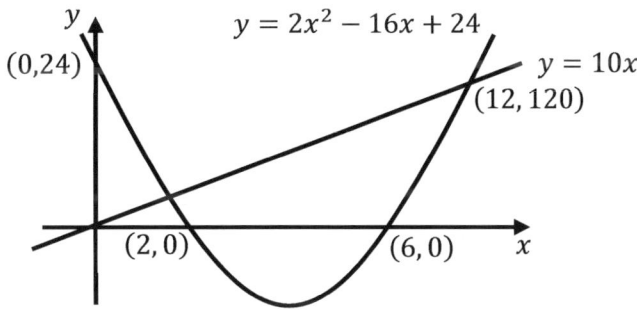

7
This is a conditional probability problem that can be represented by a probability tree.
The tree will have 3 branches in the first choice and then 9 branches for the second choice.
We are given two probabilities for successive events:
$$P(\text{red}, \text{blue}) + P(\text{blue}, \text{red}) = \frac{16}{87}$$
$$P(\text{red}, \text{red}) = \frac{28}{435}$$

We do not know the number of red or blue so if we started with the first probability there would be two unknown variables in the equation.
The second probability involves only red counters, so that means we need one unknown in the equation.
Call the number of red counters x
The probability of selecting red in the first pick will be $\frac{x}{30}$.
The probability of selecting red in the second pick will be $\frac{x-1}{29}$.
Both numerator and denominator decrease by 1 since there is one less red counter to pick from.

Probabilities in succession are multiplied so we can form and solve an equation for x:

$$P(\text{red, red}) = \frac{28}{435}$$

$$\frac{x}{30} \times \frac{x-1}{29} = \frac{28}{435} \qquad \text{Multiply numerators together.}$$

$$\frac{x(x-1)}{870} = \frac{28}{435} \qquad \begin{array}{l}\text{Multiply denominators together.}\\ \text{Multiply by 870.}\end{array}$$

$$x(x-1) = 56 \qquad \text{Expand the brackets.}$$

$$x^2 - x = 56 \qquad \text{Rearrange the quadratic to make it equal to zero.}$$

$$x^2 - x - 56 = 0 \qquad \text{Factorise.}$$

$$(x-8)(x+7) = 0 \qquad \text{Reject negative solution.}$$

Only $x = 8$ is a valid solution since x is a positive number.
There are 8 red counters.

Now we can consider the first probability given for selecting a red and blue in either order.
Call the number of blue counters y.

The probability of selecting a blue in the first pick is $\frac{y}{30}$.

The probability of selecting red, after blue, in the second pick is $\frac{8}{29}$.

The probability of selecting red in the first pick will be $\frac{8}{30}$.

The probability of selecting blue, after red, in the second pick is $\frac{y}{29}$.

Probabilities in succession are multiplied and individual outcomes are added so we can form and solve an equation for y:

$$P(\text{red, blue}) + P(\text{blue, red}) = \frac{16}{87}$$

$$\frac{8}{30} \times \frac{y}{29} + \frac{y}{30} \times \frac{8}{29} = \frac{16}{87} \qquad \begin{array}{l}\text{Multiply numerators together.}\\ \text{Multiply denominators together.}\end{array}$$

$$\frac{8y}{870} + \frac{8y}{870} = \frac{16}{87} \qquad \begin{array}{l}\text{Multiply by 870.}\\ \text{Collect the } y \text{ terms.}\end{array}$$

$$8y + 8y = 160 \qquad \text{Divide by 16.}$$

$$16y = 160$$

$$y = 10$$

There are 10 blue counters.

Now we can find the number of green counters:

$$30 - 8 - 10 = 12$$

There are 12 green counters.

The probability of selecting two green counters will be:

$$P(\text{green, green}) = \frac{12}{30} \times \frac{11}{29}$$

$$= \frac{22}{145}$$

The correct answer is $\frac{22}{145}$.

First counter   **Second counter**

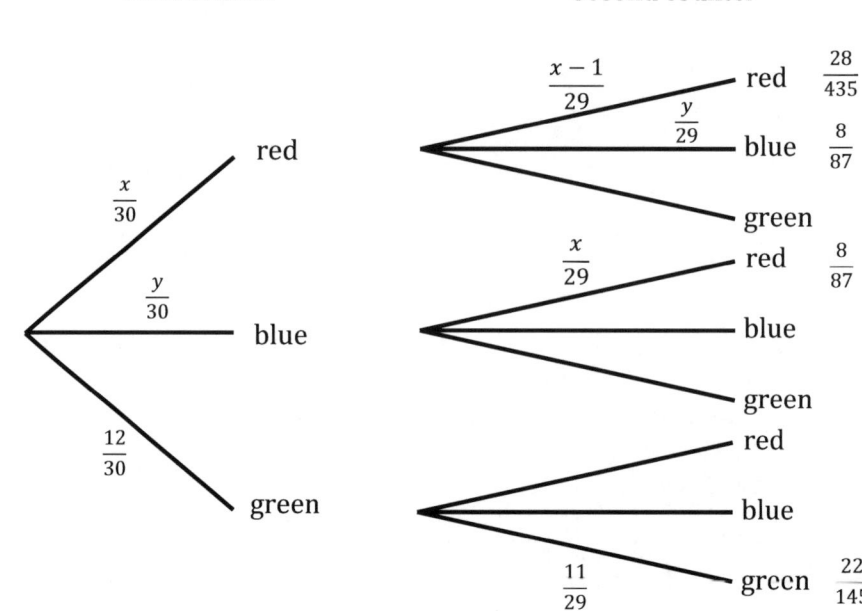

8

This is a conditional probability problem that can be represented by a probability tree.
The tree will have 3 branches in the first choice and then 9 branches for the second choice.
We are given two probabilities for successive events for different numbers of beads:

$$P(\text{red, red}) = \frac{2}{51}$$

After 6 more non-red beads are added,

$$P(\text{red, red}) = \frac{1}{46}$$

There are two unknowns here: the number of red beads and the total number of beads.
Call the original number of red beads x.
Call the original total number of beads n.
The probability of selecting a red bead from the box will be $\frac{x}{n}$.
The probability of selecting a second red bead from the box will be $\frac{x-1}{n-1}$.
We can form one equation containing x and n.
For probabilities in succession you multiply:

$$\frac{x}{n} \times \frac{x-1}{n-1} = \frac{2}{51}$$

$$\frac{x(x-1)}{n(n-1)} = \frac{2}{51} \qquad \text{Multiply the numerators and denominators together.}$$

$$51x(x-1) = 2n(n-1) \quad [1] \qquad \text{Multiply by 51 and } n(n-1).$$

Six non-red beads are added.
The probability of selecting a red bead from the box will be $\frac{x}{n+6}$.
The probability of selecting a second red bead from the box will be $\frac{x-1}{n+5}$.
We can form another equation containing x and n:

$$\frac{x}{n+6} \times \frac{x-1}{n+5} = \frac{1}{46}$$

$$\frac{x(x-1)}{(n+6)(n+5)} = \frac{1}{46} \qquad \text{Multiply the numerators and denominators together.}$$

$$46x(x-1) = (n+6)(n+5) \quad [2] \qquad \text{Multiply by 46 and } (n+6)(n+5).$$

We can now solve these simultaneous equations to find n, the original number of beads in the box.
If we eliminate all the x terms then we can solve for n.
Notice that both equation [1] and [2] contain the term $x(x-1)$.
We can make that term the subject for both equations:

$$x(x-1) = \frac{2n(n-1)}{51} \quad \text{and} \quad x(x-1) = \frac{(n+6)(n+5)}{46}$$

Therefore,

$$\frac{2n(n-1)}{51} = \frac{(n+6)(n+5)}{46}$$

$$92n(n-1) = 51(n+6)(n+5) \qquad \text{Multiply by 51 and 46.}$$

$$92n^2 - 92n = 51(n^2 + 11n + 30) \qquad \text{Expand the brackets.}$$

$$= 51n^2 + 561n + 1530 \qquad \text{Collect the terms on one side so the quadratic is set equal}$$

$$41n^2 - 653n - 1530 = 0 \qquad \text{to zero.}$$

$$(41n + 85)(n - 18) = 0 \qquad \text{Factorise or use the quadratic formula.}$$

$n = 18$ is the correct solution since n is positive.
There were originally 18 counters in the box.

If you used the quadratic formula you would get:

$$n = \frac{-b \pm \sqrt{b^2 - 4ac}}{2a}$$

$$= \frac{653 \pm \sqrt{(-653)^2 - 4(41)(-1530)}}{2(41)}$$

$$n = 18 \quad \text{or} \quad n = -\frac{85}{41}$$

Original box

$$\xrightarrow{\frac{4}{18}} \text{ red } \xrightarrow{\frac{3}{17}} \text{ red } \quad \frac{2}{51}$$

After 6 non-red beads are added

$$\xrightarrow{\frac{4}{24}} \text{ red } \xrightarrow{\frac{3}{23}} \text{ red } \quad \frac{1}{46}$$

9

This is a conditional probability problem.

We can express the scenario described with a probability tree.

The probability tree will have 2 branches for the predictions and 4 branches for the outcomes in the exam.

All the branches from a point must sum to 1.

Call the probability of predicting a pass x.

Then the probability of predicting a fail will be $1 - x$.

The probability of passing given that a pass was predicted is given as 0.9.

Then the probability of failing given that a pass was predicted is 0.1.

The probability of failing given that a fail was predicted is given as 0.7.

Then the probability of passing given that a fail was predicted is 0.3.

The probability tree shows the information.

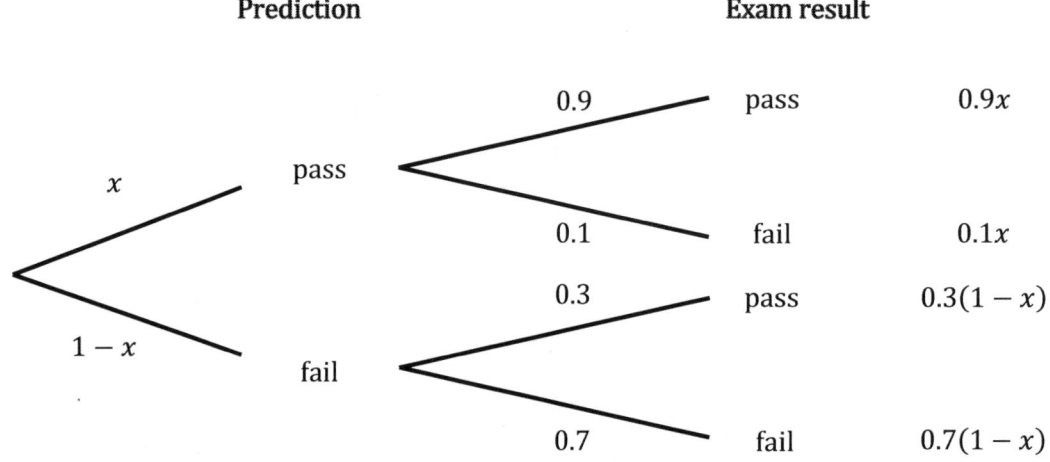

We also know the probability of passing was 0.78.

This comes from two pathways: predicted pass then pass, and predicted fail then pass.

We can form an equation and solve for x:

$$0.9x + 0.3(1 - x) = 0.78$$

$0.9x + 0.3 - 0.3x = 0.78$	Expand the brackets.
$0.6x + 0.3 = 0.78$	Simplify.
$0.6x = 0.48$	Subtract 0.3.
$x = 0.8$	Divide by 0.6.

The probability of the teacher predicting a pass is 0.8.

10

This is a conditional probability problem.

We can express the scenario described with a probability tree.

The probability tree will have 2 branches for the selection from Box A and 4 branches for the selection from Box B.

When a ball is transferred from Box A to Box B the overall number of balls will increase by 1 in Box B.

The probability tree is shown below:

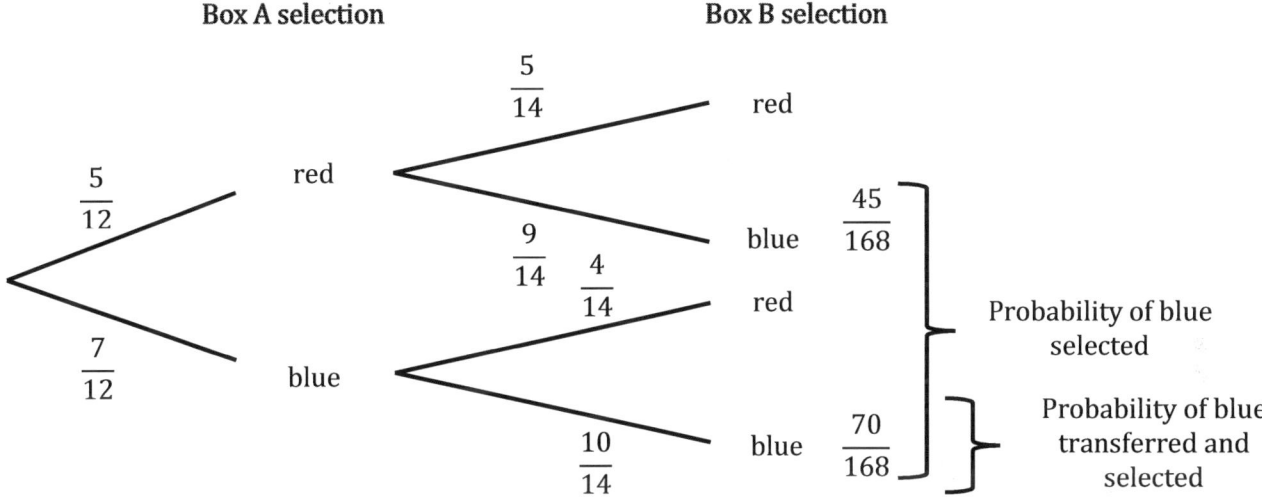

We are asked to find the probability that the ball transferred is blue given that the ball selected is blue.

This is a conditional statement which in terms of algebra would be:

$$P(\text{blue transferred given blue selected}) = \frac{\text{probability of blue transferred and blue selected}}{\text{probability of blue selected}}$$

$$= \frac{\frac{70}{168}}{\frac{45}{168} + \frac{70}{168}}$$

$$= \frac{14}{23}$$

The correct answer is $\frac{14}{23}$.

A Venn diagram can be useful in representing conditional probability.

The values in the Venn diagram below show probabilities.

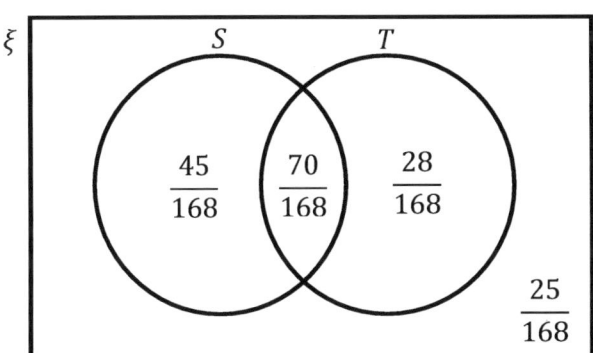

ξ represents the probabilities of the given question.

S is the probability of a blue ball being selected from Box B.

T is the probability of a blue ball being transferred from Box A.

The question can now be thought of as the following:

$$P(\text{blue transferred given blue selected}) = \frac{P(S \cap T)}{P(S)}$$

$$= \frac{\frac{70}{168}}{\frac{45}{168} + \frac{70}{168}}$$

$$= \frac{14}{23}$$

Exercise 5

1 calculator
Two motorists each travel the same 120 miles on a motorway.
The faster motorist travels 18mph quicker than the other.
The faster motorist completes the journey 90 minutes sooner than the other.
Find the speed of the slower motorist.

2 calculator
An equilateral triangle and a semicircle are shown.
The diameter of the semicircle is equal to the base length of the triangle.
The equilateral triangle has a side length of 8cm.

Show that the shaded area is equal to $8\sqrt{3} - \dfrac{8}{3}\pi$ cm^2.

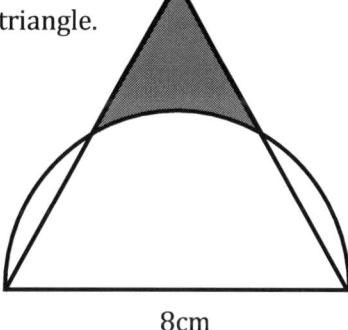

8cm

3 calculator
The populations of two colonies of bacteria are changing over time.
The population P of the first colony at time t hours is given by $P = A \times 1.1^t$
A is a constant.
The second population of bacteria is initially 50% larger than that of the first population.
The second population is decreasing by 10% every hour.
After three hours the population of the first colony has 475 more bacteria than the second colony.
Find the population of the first colony at three hours.

4
The digits 2, 3, 4, 6 and 8 can be arranged to produce five-digit numbers, e.g. 23468.
Of these five-digit numbers, 12 of them are prime numbers.
How many five-digit numbers can be produced that are not prime?

5

Forty litres of detergent are mixed with water at a factory with the ratio detergent : water $= 3 : 2$
The detergent and water are thoroughly mixed.
x litres of the mixture are removed.
x litres of detergent are added to the mixture.
The ratio is now detergent : water $= 4 : 1$
Find the value of x.

6 calculator

An experiment uses the following formula:

$$p = \frac{1}{f} - \frac{1}{u}$$

The value of p is kept constant.
The value of f when $u = 20$ is eight more than the value of f when $u = 12$.
Given that f is positive, find the value of f.

7

A 400-metre running track consists of two parallel straight sections of length x metres and two semi-circular ends.
If the distance between the parallel straight sections is 80 metres, find the value of x.

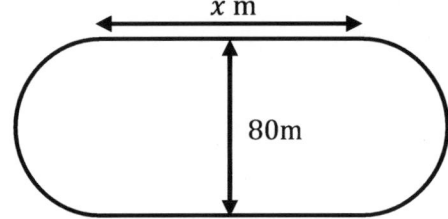

8 calculator

$$\frac{(x + 5)(12 - x)}{x + 1} = 6x$$
and
$$(a + x)(a - x) = 216$$

Find the value of a given a is an integer and $a > 0$.

9 calculator

Find three terms between 512 and 20000 so that the five terms are in a geometric sequence.

10 calculator

A circle with centre O and radius 9cm is shown.
B, A and X lie on the circumference.
OXP is a straight line and $XP = 6$cm.
BAP is a straight line and $AP = 8$cm.
Find the length of BA.

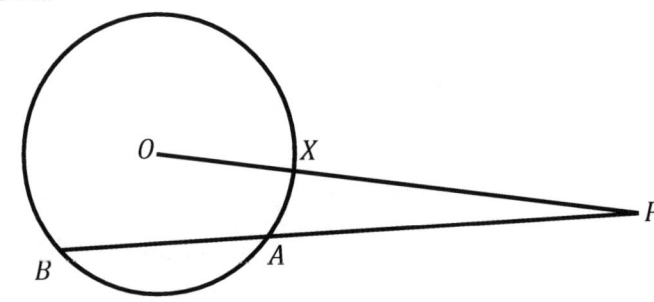

Exercise 5 Solutions

1

Call the speed of the slower motorist v mph.
The speed of the faster motorist will be $(v + 18)$ mph.
The time taken to travel the 120 miles for each motorist will be:

$$\text{faster motorist} = \frac{120}{v + 18}$$

$$\text{slower motorist} = \frac{120}{v}$$

$$\text{time} = \frac{\text{distance}}{\text{speed}}$$

We know the difference in time was 90 minutes or 1.5 hours.
We can form an equation and solve for v.

time of slower motorist $-$ time of faster motorist $= 1.5$

$$\frac{120}{v} - \frac{120}{v + 18} = 1.5 \qquad \text{Multiply by } v.$$

$$120 - \frac{120v}{v + 18} = 1.5v \qquad \text{Multiply by } (v + 18).$$

$$120(v + 18) - 120v = 1.5v(v + 18) \qquad \text{Divide by 1.5.}$$

$$80(v + 18) - 80v = v(v + 18) \qquad \text{Expand the brackets.}$$

$$80v + 1440 - 80v = v^2 + 18v \qquad \text{Simplify.}$$

$$1440 = v^2 + 18v \qquad \text{Subtract 1440.}$$

$$v^2 + 18v - 1440 = 0 \qquad \text{Set the quadratic to zero.}$$

$$(v - 30)(v + 48) = 0 \qquad \text{Factorise.}$$

$$v = 30 \text{ or } v = -48$$

Reject the negative solution.

Only $v = 30$ is valid.
Since v represented the slower speed the correct answer is 30mph.

2

The radius of the semicircle is 4cm.

Call the centre of the semicircle O.

Call the points where the semicircle intersects the triangle A and B.
$OA = 4$cm and $OB = 4$cm.
Therefore the side $AB = 4$cm.

Call the top of the triangle C.

An equilateral triangle can be split into four identical smaller equilateral triangles.
The shaded area is formed by subtracting the area of sector OAB from two equilateral triangles, each the same area as triangle ABC.
This equilateral triangle has side lengths of 4cm, so we can find its area using $\frac{1}{2}ab \sin C$.
a and b are both 4cm and the angle represented by C will be $60°$.

shaded area = 2 × equilateral triangle areas − area of sector OAB

$$= 2 \times \frac{1}{2} ab \sin C - \frac{60}{360} \times \pi r^2$$

$$= ab \sin C - \frac{1}{6} \times \pi r^2$$

$$= 4 \times 4 \times \sin 60° - \frac{1}{6} \times \pi \times 4^2$$

$$= 16 \times \frac{\sqrt{3}}{2} - \frac{16}{6} \pi$$

$$= 8\sqrt{3} - \frac{8}{3} \pi$$

This is the required answer.

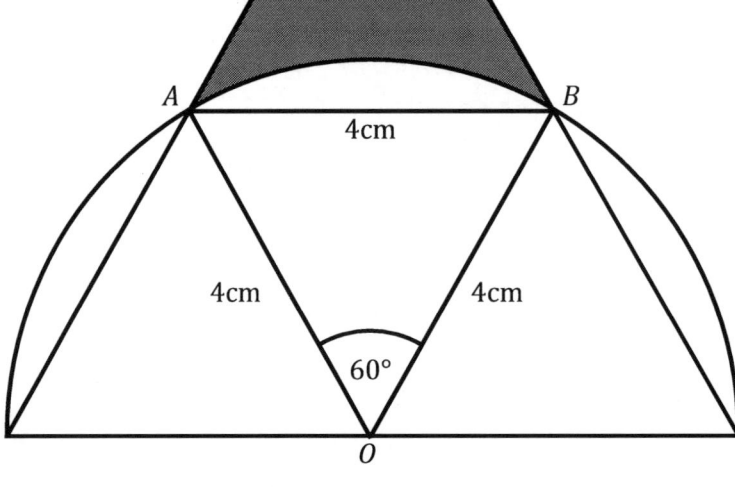

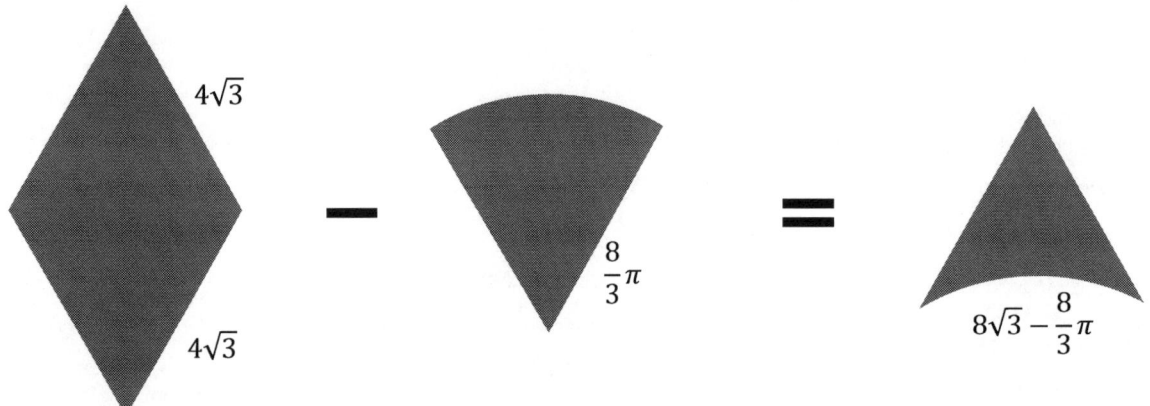

3

We have the population formula for the first colony: $P = A \times 1.1^t$

Note that in these formulae, the constant A represents the initial population.

We need to form the population formula for the second colony.

The population of the second colony is initially 50% larger; this would be $1.5A$.

It is decreasing at 10% per hour; this would be a multiplier of 0.9.

The formula for the second population will be $P = 1.5A \times 0.9^t$

After three hours each colony will have a population of:

first population $= A \times 1.1^3$

second population $= 1.5A \times 0.9^3$

We know the first population has 475 more bacteria than the second population after three hours.

This provides a link for an equation we can make and solve for A:

$$\text{first population} = \text{second population} + 475$$
$$A \times 1.1^3 = 1.5A \times 0.9^3 + 475$$
$$A \times 1.1^3 - 1.5A \times 0.9^3 = 475$$
$$A(1.1^3 - 1.5 \times 0.9^3) = 475$$
$$A = \frac{475}{1.1^3 - 1.5 \times 0.9^3}$$
$$= 2000$$

Subtract $1.5A \times 0.9^3$.
Factorise for A.
Divide by $(1.1^3 - 1.5 \times 0.9^3)$.

Now we can find the population of the first colony after three hours.

$$P = A \times 1.1^t$$
$$= 2000 \times 1.1^3$$
$$= 2662$$

The correct answer is 2662.

4

Of the five-digit numbers we can form, only numbers that end in 3 will be prime (odd numbers).
We are told that of all the different five-digit numbers, 12 are prime.
We need to find the number of ways of arranging five different digits.
This will be 120 from $5 \times 4 \times 3 \times 2 \times 1 = 120$

If 12 are prime then the remaining numbers will be non-prime.
The number of non-prime five-digit numbers will be $120 - 12 = 108$
The correct answer is 108.

Below is a table showing all the five-digit numbers that end in 3, and whether they are prime.

24683	Prime	42683	Prime	62483	Prime	82463	Prime
24863		42863	Prime	62843		82643	
26483		46823		64283	Prime	84263	Prime
26843		46283		64823		84623	
28463	Prime	48263		68243		86243	Prime
28643	Prime	48623	Prime	68423		86423	Prime

5

For this question we need to keep a running total of the volume of detergent and water in the mixture.
These totals will involve the variable x.
If the detergent and water are thoroughly mixed then when any of the mixture is removed, the amount
removed of detergent or water will be proportional to their relative volumes.
For example,
Say you had 100L of which 80L were detergent and 20L were water and you mixed them together.
If you then removed half the mixture you would remove half of each of the detergent and water.
There would now be 40L of detergent and 10L of water.
We have 40L of mixture split into the ratio detergent : water $= 3 : 2$
This means we have 24L of detergent and 16L of water.
Now x litres of mixture are removed.
Since $\frac{3}{5}$ of the mixture is detergent, $\frac{3}{5}x$ will be the amount of detergent removed.
Since $\frac{2}{5}$ of the mixture is water, $\frac{2}{5}x$ will be the amount of water removed.

So we now have the ratio detergent : water $= 24 - \frac{3}{5}x : 16 - \frac{2}{5}x$

Now x litres of detergent are added to the mixture.

We now have $\left(24 - \frac{3}{5}x + x\right)$ litres of detergent.

So we now have the ratio detergent : water $= 24 - \frac{3}{5}x + x : 16 - \frac{2}{5}x$

We know that this ratio is equivalent to $4 : 1$.

This allows us to cross multiply the ratio to form and solve an equation for x.

$$24 - \frac{3}{5}x + x : 16 - \frac{2}{5}x = 4 : 1$$

$24 + \frac{2}{5}x : 16 - \frac{2}{5}x = 4 : 1$ Simplify $-\frac{3}{5}x + x$ into $\frac{2}{5}x$.

$\dfrac{120 + 2x}{5} : \dfrac{80 - 2x}{5} = 4 : 1$ Write the left ratio over the common denominator 5.

$120 + 2x : 80 - 2x = 4 : 1$ Multiply by 5.

Cross multiplying a ratio

$120 + 2x : 80 - 2x$

$4 : 1$

$4(80 - 2x) = 120 + 2x$

Using ratio cross multiplication:

$4(80 - 2x) = 120 + 2x$ Multiply out the brackets.

$320 - 8x = 120 + 2x$ Add $8x$.

$200 = 10x$ Subtract 120.

$x = 20$ Divide by 10.

The correct answer is $x = 20$.

6

p is a constant so it will be unaffected by the changes in the variables u and f.

The value of f when $u = 20$ is eight more than the value of f when $u = 12$.

This describes two scenarios:

$u = 20$ and $f = f + 8$

$u = 12$ and $f = f$

We can form two equations:

$$p = \frac{1}{f + 8} - \frac{1}{20} \quad [1]$$

$$p = \frac{1}{f} - \frac{1}{12} \quad [2]$$

$$p = \frac{1}{f} - \frac{1}{u}$$

Since p is constant we can say the right hand side of equations [1] and [2] are equal.

We can then solve for f.

$$\frac{1}{f} - \frac{1}{12} = \frac{1}{f + 8} - \frac{1}{20}$$

$\dfrac{1}{f} - \dfrac{1}{30} = \dfrac{1}{f + 8}$ Add $\frac{1}{20}$.

$1 - \dfrac{f}{30} = \dfrac{f}{f + 8}$ Multiply by f.

$f + 8 - \dfrac{f(f + 8)}{30} = f$ Multiply by $(f + 8)$.

$30(f + 8) - f(f + 8) = 30f$ Multiply by 30.

$30f + 240 - f^2 - 8f = 30f$ Multiply out the brackets.

$240 - f^2 - 8f = 0$ Cancel the $30f$ from both sides.

$f^2 + 8f - 240 = 0$ Form a quadratic set equal to zero and factorise.

$(f + 20)(f - 12) = 0$ Reject the negative solution.

f is a positive value so the correct answer is $f = 12$.

7

The perimeter of the track is formed from two semicircles (which make a full circumference) and two straight sections of length x.

Since 80m separate the parallel sections we know that the diameter of the circle is 80m.

The circumference of the circle will be $\pi d = 80\pi$ metres.

We can now form and solve an equation for x.

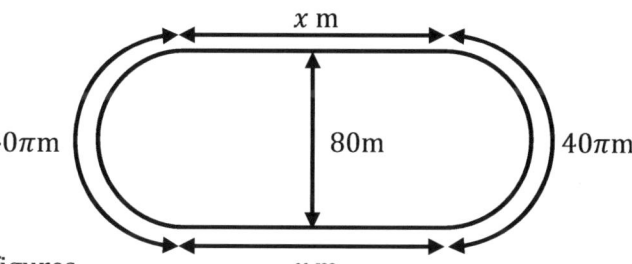

perimeter $= 400$

$80\pi + 2x = 400$

$2x = 400 - 80\pi$ Subtract 80π.

$x = 200 - 40\pi$ Divide by 2.

$= 74.336\ldots$

The value of x is 74.3 metres correct to three significant figures.

8

We need to find the value of x in the first equation and then substitute this value into the second equation to find a.

$$\frac{(x+5)(12-x)}{x+1} = 6x$$

$(x+5)(12-x) = 6x(x+1)$ Multiply by $(x+1)$.

$12x - x^2 + 60 - 5x = 6x^2 + 6x$ Expand the brackets.

$7x^2 - x - 60 = 0$ Collect the terms and form a quadratic set equal to zero.

$(7x + 20)(x - 3) = 0$ Factorise.

$x = -\dfrac{20}{7}$ or $x = 3$

If we examine the second equation we can see that it forms the difference of two squares:

$(a+x)(a-x) = a^2 - x^2$

First we substitute $x = -\frac{20}{7}$:

$a^2 - x^2 = 216$

$a^2 - \left(-\dfrac{20}{7}\right)^2 = 216$

$a^2 - \dfrac{400}{49} = 216$

$a^2 = \dfrac{10984}{49}$

$a = 14.97\ldots$

This is not an integer.

Now we substitute $x = 3$:

$a^2 - x^2 = 216$

$a^2 - 3^2 = 216$

$a^2 = 225$

$a = 15$

$a = 15$ is the correct answer.

We did not require the negative square root since a was positive.

9

A geometric sequence is formed by multiplying successive terms by a constant value.

We will call this value r.

The first term is 512.
The fifth term is 20000.
The second term would be $512r$.
The third term $512r^2$.
The fourth term $512r^3$.
For the fifth term we can form an equation and solve for r.
$512r^4 = 20000$
$\qquad r^4 = 39.0625 \qquad$ Divide by 512.
$\qquad r = 2.5 \qquad$ Take the fourth root: $39.0625^{0.25}$.

Note that we do not require $r = -2.5$ since all the terms of the sequence are positive.
We now generate the other terms:
$512 \times 2.5 = 1280$
$1280 \times 2.5 = 3200$
$3200 \times 2.5 = 8000$

The correct answer is 1280, 3200, and 8000.

10
The radius of the circle is 9cm.
This means OX, OA and OB are all 9cm since they are radii.
The length $OP = 15$cm.
We know two lengths of the triangle OBP: 15cm and 9cm.
Let $BA = x$.
The third side of triangle OBP is $BP = x + 8$.
We need to know a mixture of 3 angles and sides in a triangle before we can determine other angles and sides.
Notice that the triangle OAP and OBP share the angle OPB.
We know three sides of the triangle OAP.
This allows us to calculate the angle OPB using the cosine rule:
$$a^2 = b^2 + c^2 - 2bc \cos A$$
$$OA^2 = OP^2 + AP^2 - 2(OP)(AP)\cos(OPB)$$
$$9^2 = 15^2 + 8^2 - 2(15)(8)\cos(OPB)$$
$$81 = 225 + 64 - 240\cos(OPB)$$
$$-208 = -240\cos(OPB)$$
$$\cos(OPB) = \frac{13}{15}$$

Keep this angle exact for now.
Now we can use the cosine rule with triangle OBP:
$$a^2 = b^2 + c^2 - 2bc \cos A$$
$$OB^2 = OP^2 + BP^2 - 2(OP)(BP)\cos(OPB)$$
$$9^2 = 15^2 + (x+8)^2 - 2(15)(x+8)\left(\frac{13}{15}\right)$$
$$81 = 225 + (x+8)(x+8) - 26(x+8)$$
$$81 = 225 + x^2 + 8x + 8x + 64 - 26x - 208$$
$$x^2 - 10x = 0$$
$$x(x - 10) = 0$$
$$x = 0 \text{ or } x = 10$$
Only $x = 10$ is valid.

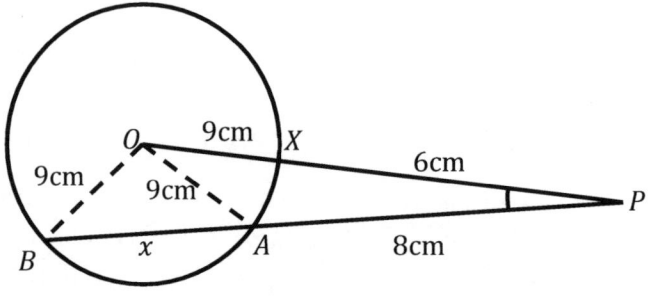

The correct answer is $x = 10$ (BA is 10cm).

Exercise 6

1

A rectangle $ABCD$ is shown with another identical rectangle $AEFG$.

Rectangle $AEFG$ is a rotation of rectangle $ABCD$ at $30°$ to the horizontal with the point A fixed.

Side $AB = 8$cm and side $AD = 5$cm.

Find the value of $\frac{EB^2}{BG}$ written in surd form.

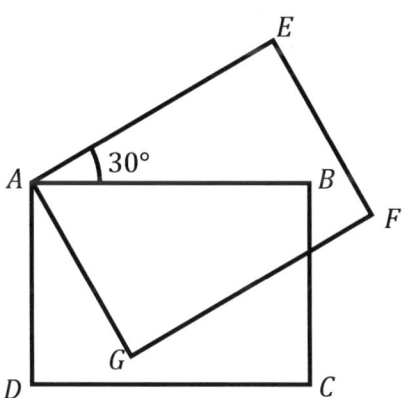

2 calculator

Triangle ABC has side lengths:

$AB = 40$cm

$BC = 26$cm

$AC = 42$cm

D is a point on the side AC.

BD is perpendicular to AC.

Find the length of BD.

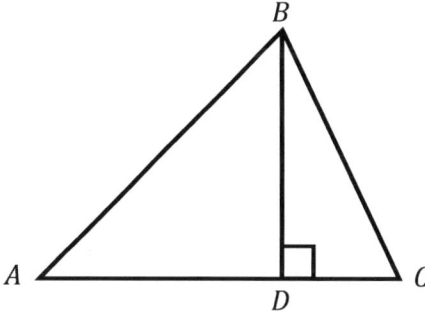

3

A box in the shape of a cuboid has length a, width b and depth c.

Find the length of the longest object that can fit into the box in terms of a, b and c.

4

ACB is a straight line.
ABD and *ACE* are equilateral triangles.
Prove that $CD = BE$

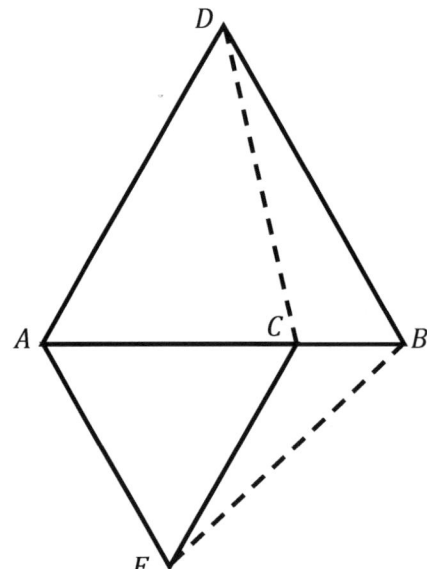

5 calculator

A company owns a factory producing radiators.

In the first year of manufacture:
The cost price of the raw materials is £54 per radiator.
The selling price is £*x* per radiator.
75000 radiators are sold.
The running cost of the factory is £5265000.
The profit is £*y*.

In the second year of manufacture:
The cost price increases by £3 per radiator.
The selling price increases by £22 per radiator.
18462 fewer radiators are sold.
The running costs decrease by 20%.
The profit increases by 78%.

Find the value of *x*.

6

ABCD is a quadrilateral with sides $BC = \left(10\sqrt{3} - 5\right)$ cm, $AD = \left(10 - 5\sqrt{3}\right)$ cm and $AB = 20$ cm.
Angle $BAD = 60°$ and angle $ABC = 30°$.
Would the points A, B, C and D all lie on the circumference of the same circle?
Give reasons for your answer.

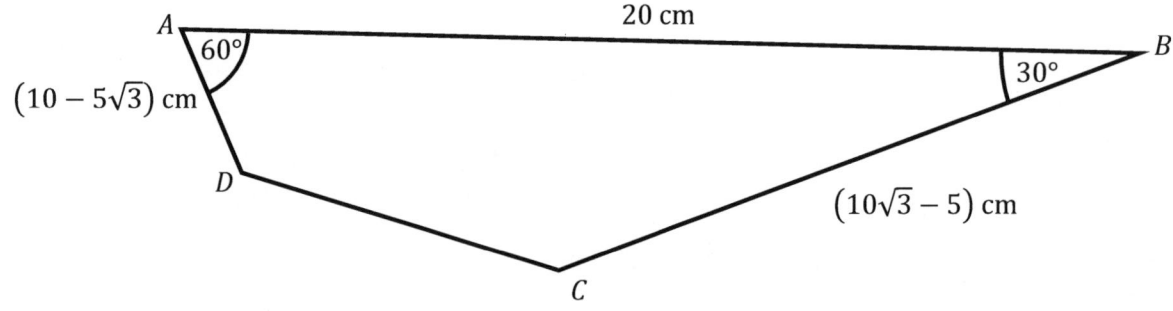

7 calculator

A car passes a point A at a speed of 16m/s and immediately accelerates.
The car accelerates at a constant rate to 32m/s.
24 seconds later a motorcycle sets off from rest at point A and accelerates at a constant rate until it overtakes the car.
120 seconds after the car passes point A the car and motorcycle have travelled equal distances from point A.
Find how many seconds after the motorcycle set off that the car and motorcycle were travelling at the same speed.
Give your answer in seconds as a mixed number.

8 calculator

Rectangle $ABCD$ is shown split into three triangles.
E lies on the line AD.
The ratio $BC : BA = \sqrt{3} : 1$ in the rectangle.
Triangles ABE and BED are equal in area.
Find the ratio of the lengths $BE : BD$ in the form $\sqrt{a} : b$
where a and b are integers in their simplest form.

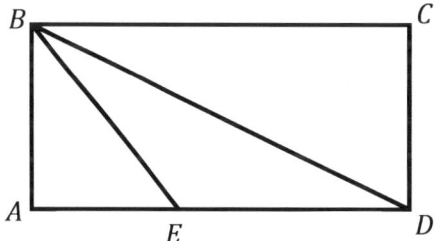

9 calculator

Two groups of different supercomputers are able to decode encrypted messages.
Each group is set a task of decoding 40 messages.

In the first group,
x computers operate for 60 minutes and decode 30 messages.
Then $x + 6$ computers decode the rest of the messages.

In the second group,
$(2x + 4)$ computers operate for 45 minutes and decode 10 messages.
Then $(2x - 6)$ computers decode the rest of the messages.

The first group decoded the 40 messages in $\frac{1}{3}$ of the time of the second group.
Assume the computers within each group all work at the same rate.
How many times faster is a computer from the first group than a computer from the second group?

10 calculator

A quarter circle is shown inside the square $ABCD$.
The circle has a radius of 8cm.
A square, $DEFG$ also touches the quarter circle at F and shares two sides with the square $ABCD$.
Find the length of EG in the form $a + b\sqrt{c}$.

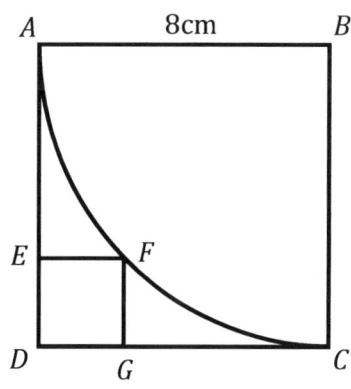

Exercise 6 Solutions

1

EB forms part of the triangle AEB.

We know $AB = 8$cm, $AE = 8$cm and the angle $EAB = 30°$

This produces an "angle sandwich" which means we can use the cosine rule to calculate EB^2:

$$a^2 = b^2 + c^2 - 2bc \cos A$$
$$EB^2 = AB^2 + AE^2 - 2(AB)(AE) \cos 30°$$
$$EB^2 = 8^2 + 8^2 - 2 \times 8 \times 8 \times \cos 30°$$
$$= 64 + 64 - 128 \times \frac{\sqrt{3}}{2} \qquad \cos 30° = \frac{\sqrt{3}}{2}$$
$$= 128 - 64\sqrt{3}$$

BG forms part of the triangle ABG.

We know $AB = 8$cm, $AG = 5$cm and the angle $BAG = 60°$

(Angle $BAG = 60°$ because it forms part of the right angle with angle EAB).

This produces an "angle sandwich" which means we can use the cosine rule to calculate BG:

$$a^2 = b^2 + c^2 - 2bc \cos A$$
$$BG^2 = AB^2 + AG^2 - 2(AB)(AG) \cos 60°$$
$$BG^2 = 8^2 + 5^2 - 2 \times 8 \times 5 \times \cos 60°$$
$$= 64 + 25 - 80 \times \frac{1}{2} \qquad \cos 60° = \frac{1}{2}$$
$$= 89 - 40$$
$$= 49$$
$$BG = 7$$

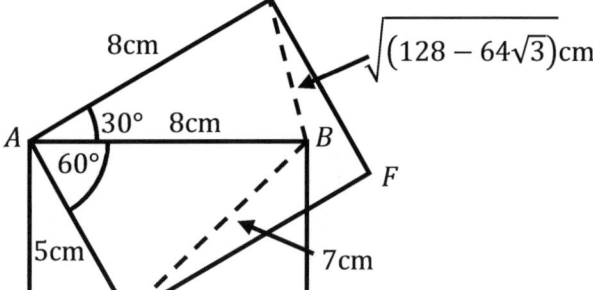

Now we can find the value of $\frac{EB^2}{BG}$:

$$\frac{EB^2}{BG} = \frac{128 - 64\sqrt{3}}{7}$$

2

Let $BD = h$cm

Let $DC = x$cm

We can use Pythagoras on triangle ABD:

$$a^2 + b^2 = c^2$$
$$AD^2 + BD^2 = AB^2$$
$$(42 - x)^2 + h^2 = 40^2$$
$$(42 - x)(42 - x) + h^2 = 1600$$
$$1764 - 42x - 42x + x^2 + h^2 = 1600$$
$$164 - 84x + x^2 + h^2 = 0 \quad [1]$$

We can use Pythagoras on triangle BCD:

$$a^2 + b^2 = c^2$$
$$BD^2 + DC^2 = BC^2$$
$$h^2 + x^2 = 26^2$$
$$h^2 + x^2 = 676 \quad [2]$$

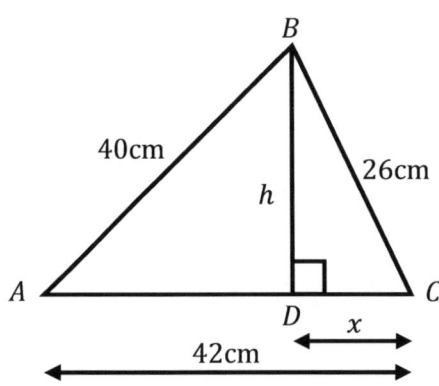

We can substitute equation [2] into equation [1]:
$$164 - 84x + 676 = 0$$
$$84x = 840$$
$$x = 10$$

We substitute $x = 10$ into equation [2]:
$$h^2 + 10^2 = 676$$
$$h^2 + 100 = 676$$
$$h^2 = 576$$
$$h = 24$$

The correct answer is $BD = 24$cm.

3
The longest object to fit into a cuboid will be along the lead diagonal.
Call the lead diagonal d.
Call the diagonal of the base rectangle e.

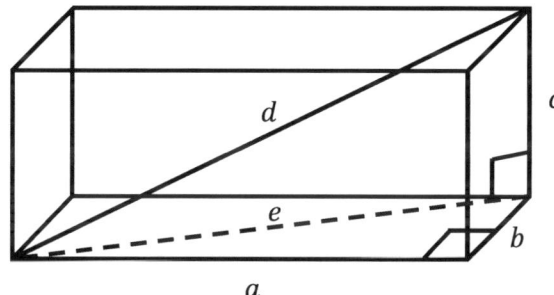

The base of a cuboid is a rectangle which can be split into two right-angled triangles.
We can use Pythagoras to connect the sides:
$$a^2 + b^2 = e^2 \quad [1]$$

The triangle with sides c, d and e is also right-angled, so again using Pythagoras:
$$e^2 + c^2 = d^2 \quad [2]$$

We can substitute equation [1] into equation [2]:
$$a^2 + b^2 + c^2 = d^2$$

We can make d the subject by taking the square root:
$$d = \sqrt{a^2 + b^2 + c^2}$$

The correct answer is the length of the longest object that can fit into a cuboid of lengths a, b and c is:
$$\sqrt{a^2 + b^2 + c^2}$$

4
We know that triangles ABD and ACE are equilateral.
Their respective sides will be the same length and each interior angle will be $60°$.
Since ACB is a straight line we know angle $BCE = 120°$.
We need to prove $CD = BE$ so we require two equations that contain each of these side lengths.
If CD and BE are equal to the same value then they must both be equal to each other.

We can start by using the cosine rule on the triangle ACD:
$$a^2 = b^2 + c^2 - 2bc \cos A$$
$$CD^2 = AD^2 + AC^2 - 2(AD)(AC) \cos 60°$$
$$= AD^2 + AC^2 - (AD)(AC) \quad [1]$$

$$\cos 60° = \frac{1}{2}$$

Now we apply the cosine rule to triangle BCE:
$$a^2 = b^2 + c^2 - 2bc \cos A$$
$$BE^2 = BC^2 + CE^2 - 2(BC)(CE) \cos 120°$$
$$= BC^2 + CE^2 + (BC)(CE) \quad [2]$$

$$\cos 120° = -\frac{1}{2}$$

We have two equations with both CD and BE.
Note that $AB = AC + BC$
And also,
$AC = CE$
We can replace BC with $AB - AC$ in equation [2].
We can replace CE with AC in equation [2].

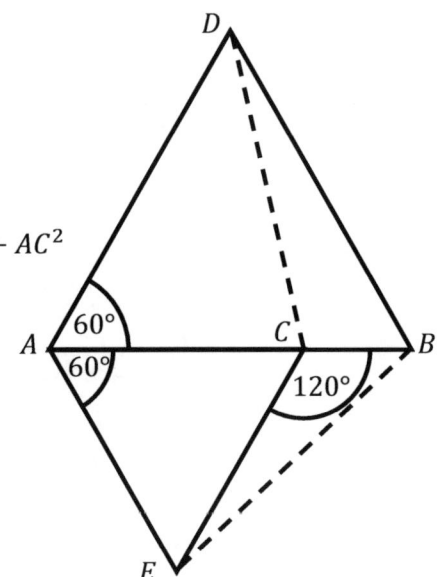

With these substitutions we obtain:
$$BE^2 = BC^2 + CE^2 + (BC)(CE)$$
$$BE^2 = (AB - AC)^2 + AC^2 + (AB - AC)(AC)$$
$$= (AB - AC)(AB - AC) + AC^2 + (AB)(AC) - AC^2$$
$$= AB^2 - (AB)(AC) - (AB)(AC) + AC^2 + AC^2 + (AB)(AC) - AC^2$$
$$= AB^2 - (AB)(AC) + AC^2$$
$$= AB^2 + AC^2 - (AB)(AC)$$

We also know $AB = AD$
So we now get
$$BE^2 = AB^2 + AC^2 - (AB)(AC)$$
$$= AD^2 + AC^2 - (AD)(AC)$$

The right hand side is identical to equation [1].
Therefore,
$$CD^2 = BE^2$$
$$CD = BE$$
This completes the proof.

5
We can represent the data provided for the two years in a table.
The second year cost price will be $54 + 3 = 57$.
The second year selling price will be $x + 22$.
The second year quantity of radiators sold will be $75000 - 18462 = 56538$.
The second year running costs will be $5265000 \times 0.8 = 4212000$.
The second year profit will be $y \times 1.78 = 1.78y$

	Cost price	Selling price	Quantity	Running costs	Profit
First year	£54	£x	75000	£5265000	£y
Second year	£57	£$(x + 22)$	56538	£4212000	£$1.78y$

We now need to form two equations to solve for x and y.
We can use the profit equation: profit = income − expenses
The income is from the sale of the radiators.
The expenses are from the purchase of raw materials for the radiators and the running costs.

For the first year:
profit = income − expenses
$$y = 75000 \times x - 75000 \times 54 - 5265000$$
$$= 75000x - 4050000 - 5265000$$
$$= 75000x - 9315000 \quad [1]$$

For the second year:
profit = income − expenses

$1.78y = 56538(x + 22) - 56538 \times 57 - 4212000$	Expand the brackets.
$= 56538x + 1243836 - 3222666 - 4212000$	Simplify.
$= 56538x - 6190830 \quad [2]$	

We have two equations containing x and y.

Substituting equation [1] into equation [2] we obtain:	Substitute $y = 75000x - 9315000$ into
$1.78(75000x - 9315000) = 56538x - 6190830$	equation [2]
$133500x - 16580700 = 56538x - 6190830$	Expand the brackets.
$76962x = 10389870$	Add 16580700 and subtract $56538x$.
$x = 135$	Divide by 76962.

The original selling price of a radiator was £135.

6

If all the points A, B, C and D lie on the circumference of the same circle then $ABCD$ must be a cyclic quadrilateral.
The opposite angles in a cyclic quadrilateral sum to 180°.
This would mean angle $ADC = 150°$ and angle $DCB = 120°$.
We need to show whether angle $ADC = 150°$ and angle $DCB = 120°$ is correct.
We can extend the sides AD and BC until they meet.
Call this point E.
The angle $AEB = 90°$ since the other two angles, EAB and ABE are 60° and 30° respectively.
If triangle AEB is right-angled we can use trigonometry SOHCAHTOA to find the lengths of the sides AE and EB.

To find side AE:
$$\sin 30° = \frac{\text{opposite}}{\text{hypotenuse}}$$
$$= \frac{AE}{AB}$$
$$= \frac{AE}{20}$$
$$AE = 20 \sin 30°$$
$$= 10 \qquad \sin 30° = \frac{1}{2}$$

To find side EB:
$$\cos 30° = \frac{\text{adjacent}}{\text{hypotenuse}}$$
$$= \frac{EB}{20}$$
$$EB = 20 \cos 30°$$
$$= 10\sqrt{3} \qquad \cos 30° = \frac{\sqrt{3}}{2}$$

We can now find the sides DE and EC:

$DE = AE - AD$

$\quad = 10 - \left(10 - 5\sqrt{3}\right)$ Expand the brackets.

$\quad = 10 - 10 + 5\sqrt{3}$ Simplify.

$\quad = 5\sqrt{3}$

$EC = EB - CB$

$\quad = 10\sqrt{3} - \left(10\sqrt{3} - 5\right)$

$\quad = 10\sqrt{3} - 10\sqrt{3} + 5$ Expand the brackets.

$\quad = 5$ Simplify.

We know the triangle DEC is right-angled.
We can use trigonometry SOHCAHTOA to find the sizes of angles EDC and DCE.

$\tan EDC = \dfrac{\text{opposite}}{\text{adjacent}}$

$\qquad\quad = \dfrac{EC}{DE}$

$\qquad\quad = \dfrac{5}{5\sqrt{3}}$

$\qquad\quad = \dfrac{1}{\sqrt{3}}$ Cancel the 5's on the numerator and denominator.

angle $EDC = \tan^{-1}\dfrac{1}{\sqrt{3}}$ $\tan 30° = \dfrac{1}{\sqrt{3}}$

$\qquad\qquad = 30°$

Since there are 180° in a triangle we know angle $DCE = 60°$
Now we can find the other two angles in the quadrilateral $ABCD$

angle $ADC = 180° - 30°$

$\qquad\qquad = 150°$

angle $DCB = 180° - 60°$

$\qquad\qquad = 120°$

The quadrilateral is cyclic.
The points A, B, C and D lie on the circumference of the same circle.

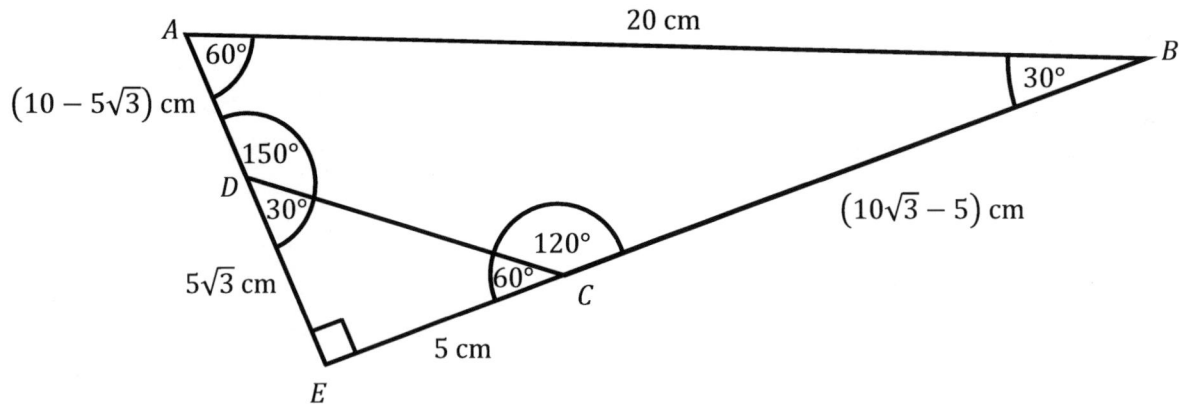

7

We need to draw a velocity-time graph to represent the motion of the car and motorcycle (see below).
Call the final velocity reached by the motorcycle vm/s.
The area under the graph for the car and motorcycle will be the same at the point when the motorcycle overtakes the car.
This will be at 120 seconds since the car and motorcycle have travelled the same distance at this time.

The shape for the car is a trapezium:

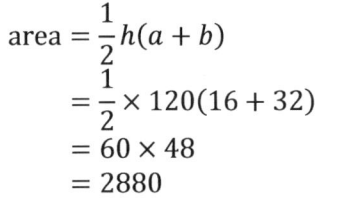

$$\text{area} = \frac{1}{2}h(a + b)$$
$$= \frac{1}{2} \times 120(16 + 32)$$
$$= 60 \times 48$$
$$= 2880$$

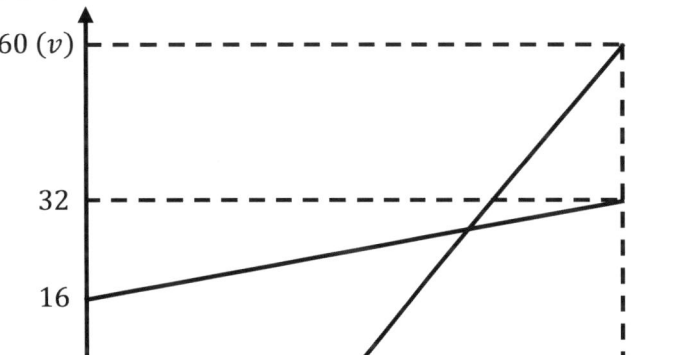

The shape for the motorcycle is a triangle:
$$\text{area} = \frac{1}{2}bh$$
$$= \frac{1}{2} \times (120 - 24) \times v$$
$$= 48v$$

We equate the areas to find v:
$$48v = 2880$$
$$v = 60$$

The motorcycle speed when it overtook the car was 60m/s.
We need to find the time from when the motorcycle set off to when it was travelling at the same speed as the car.
This can be found if we think of each of the two lines as equations for velocity and time.
For each line we need the gradient (acceleration) and the point where the line crosses the velocity axis.

For the car the gradient can be found using the start and end velocity with their associated times:
$$\text{gradient for car} = \frac{32 - 16}{120 - 0}$$
$$= \frac{16}{120}$$
$$= \frac{2}{15}$$

The car starts at 16m/s so we can say the equation for the car will be:
$$v = \frac{2}{15}t + 16$$

For the motorcycle:
$$\text{gradient for motorcycle} = \frac{60 - 0}{120 - 24}$$
$$= \frac{60}{96}$$
$$= \frac{5}{8}$$

To find the velocity axis intercept we need to substitute a point on the motorcycle line (24,0) into a generalised line equation.

Call the point where the motorcycle line crosses the velocity axis c.

Then we can write:

$$v = \frac{5}{8}t + c$$
$$0 = \frac{5}{8}(24) + c$$
$$= 15 + c$$
$$c = -15$$

The velocity intercept is -15.

The equation for the motorcycle will be:

$$v = \frac{5}{8}t - 15$$

We can now set both equations equal to each other to find the time when the velocity was the same for both the car and motorcycle:

$$\frac{5}{8}t - 15 = \frac{2}{15}t + 16$$

$$\frac{59}{120}t - 15 = 16 \qquad \text{Subtract } \frac{2}{15}t.$$

$$\frac{59}{120}t = 31 \qquad \text{Add 15.}$$

$$t = 63\frac{3}{59} \qquad \text{Divide by } \frac{59}{120}.$$

This time is how long after the car passed point A.

To find how many seconds after the motorcycle set off we subtract 24:

$$63\frac{3}{59} - 24 = 39\frac{3}{59}$$

The correct answer is $39\frac{3}{59}$ seconds.

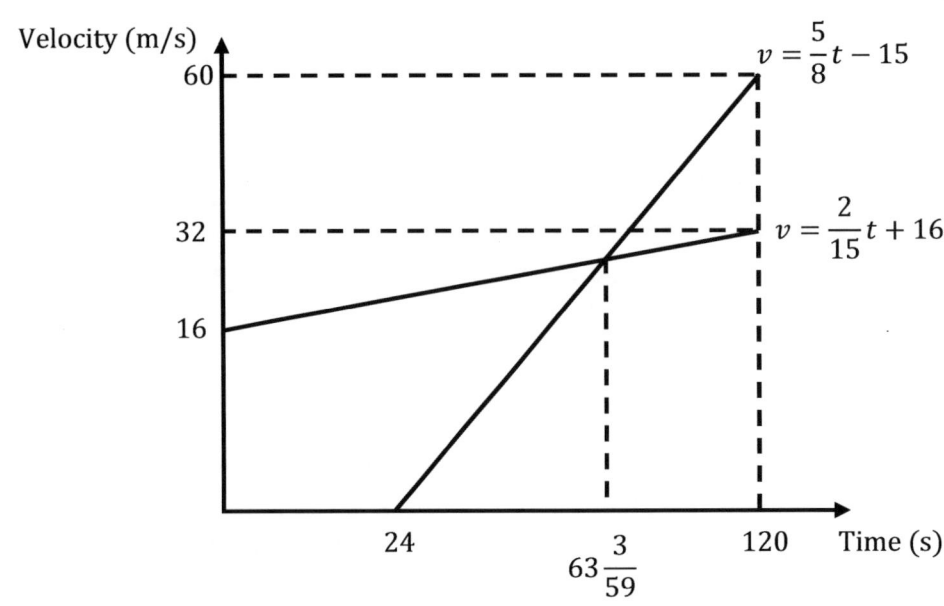

8

This question uses ratio so we can let the sides $AB = 1$ and $BC = \sqrt{3}$

As ratios are measures of proportion we can select any lengths we like as long as the ratio is maintained.

Notice that triangles ABE and BED have the same height (the same as the width of the rectangle).

If their areas are the same then the base length must be the same such that $AE : ED = 1 : 1$

This ratio splits a side AD that is $\sqrt{3}$ units in length.

So the length of $AE = \dfrac{\sqrt{3}}{2}$

We can use Pythagoras on triangle ABE to find the length of BE.

$$AB^2 + AE^2 = BE^2$$

$$1^2 + \left(\frac{\sqrt{3}}{2}\right)^2 = BE^2$$

$$1 + \frac{3}{4} = BE^2$$

$$BE^2 = \frac{7}{4}$$

$$BE = \frac{\sqrt{7}}{2}$$

The length BD is the diagonal of the rectangle so we can use Pythagoras again:

$$BC^2 + CD^2 = BD^2$$

$$\left(\sqrt{3}\right)^2 + 1^2 = BD^2$$

$$3 + 1 = BD^2$$

$$BD = 2$$

Now we can form the ratio $BE : BD$

$$BE : BD = \frac{\sqrt{7}}{2} : 2$$

$$= \sqrt{7} : 4 \qquad \text{Multiply by 2.}$$

The correct answer is $\sqrt{7} : 4$

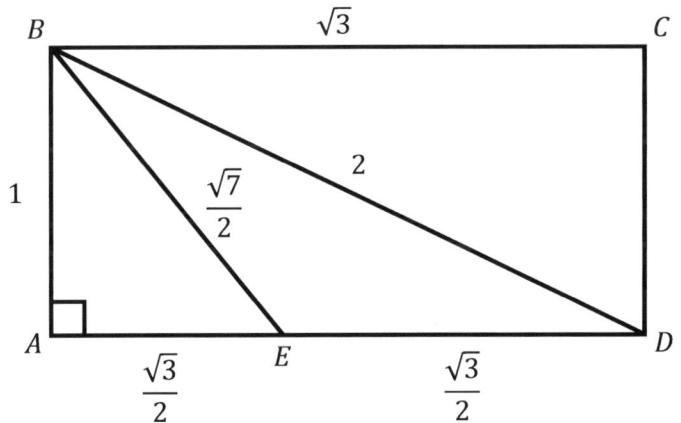

9

We can measure the speed of the computers using the units "messages per computer per minute".

This will be calculated as follows:

$$\text{speed of computers} = \frac{\text{messages}}{\text{computers} \times \text{minutes}}$$

We need the value of x to measure the speed.

This question is based on variation.

There are three variables: computers, messages and time.

You must always check how the variables are proportionally related.

Computers and messages are directly proportional: more computers mean more messages decoded.

Computers and time are inversely proportional: more computers would require less time to decode the messages.

Messages and time are directly proportional: more messages would take more time to decode.

There are two groups described in the question.

Both decode 40 messages.

The second group takes 3 times as long as the first group.

A table showing the proportional changes will be helpful.

Start with the input values given in the question.

For the first group:

Computers	Messages	Time	
x	30	60	
$x + 6$	30	$\dfrac{60x}{x + 6}$	*Computers multiplied by $\dfrac{x+6}{x}$ Time multiplied by $\dfrac{x}{x+6}$
$x + 6$	10	$\dfrac{20x}{x + 6}$	Messages and time both divided by 3.

Note that the first group had decoded 30 of the 40 messages in 60 minutes, so there were 10 left.

*Remember with proportion that to find a multiplier you divide where you are going by where you came from.

The computers had increased from x to $x + 6$ so the multiplier is found by:

$$\text{multiplier} = \frac{\text{where you are going}}{\text{where you came from}}$$
$$= \frac{x + 6}{x}$$

However, computers and time are inversely proportional, so time was multiplied by $\dfrac{x}{x+6}$.

The total time taken by the first group (in minutes) was:

$$\frac{20x}{x + 6} + 60$$

For the second group:

Computers	Messages	Time	
$2x + 4$	10	45	
$2x - 6$	10	$\dfrac{45(2x + 4)}{2x - 6}$	Computers multiplied by $\dfrac{2x-6}{2x+4}$ **Time multiplied by $\dfrac{2x+4}{2x-6}$
$2x - 6$	30	$\dfrac{135(2x + 4)}{2x - 6}$	Messages and time both multiplied by 3.

Note that the second group had decoded 10 of the 40 messages in 45 minutes, so there were 30 left.

**Again, computers and time are inversely proportional so time was multiplied by $\frac{2x+4}{2x-6}$.

The total time taken by the second group (in minutes) was:
$$\frac{135(2x+4)}{2x-6}+45$$

We know that the second group took 3 times as long as the first group, so we can say:

second group time $= 3 \times$ first group time

$$\frac{135(2x+4)}{2x-6}+45=3\left(\frac{20x}{x+6}+60\right)$$ Cancel a factor of 2 from $(2x+4)$ on the numerator and $(2x-6)$ on the denominator.

$$\frac{135(x+2)}{x-3}+45=3\left(\frac{20x}{x+6}+60\right)$$ Expand the brackets on the right hand side.

$$\frac{135(x+2)}{x-3}+45=\frac{60x}{x+6}+180$$ Subtract 45.

$$\frac{135(x+2)}{x-3}=\frac{60x}{x+6}+135$$ Multiply by $(x+6)$.

Multiply by $(x-3)$.

$$\frac{135(x+2)(x+6)}{x-3}=60x+135(x+6)$$ Divide by 15.

Expand the brackets.

$$135(x+2)(x+6)=60x(x-3)+135(x+6)(x-3)$$ Cancel the $9x^2$ from both sides.

$$9(x+2)(x+6)=4x(x-3)+9(x+6)(x-3)$$ Collect the terms so the quadratic is set equal to zero.

$$9(x^2+6x+2x+12)=4x^2-12x+9(x^2-3x+6x-18)$$ Factorise or use the quadratic formula:

$$9x^2+72x+108=4x^2-12x+9x^2+27x-162$$

$$72x+108=4x^2+15x-162$$ $$x=\frac{-b\pm\sqrt{b^2-4ac}}{2a}$$

$$4x^2-57x-270=0$$ x must be positive.

$$(4x+15)(x-18)=0$$

$x=18$ is the correct solution since x must be an integer.

Now we can calculate the speed of the computers in each group.
We can use the values from the first row in each table:

$$\text{speed of computers in first group}=\frac{\text{messages}}{\text{computers}\times\text{minutes}}$$
$$=\frac{30}{18\times60}$$
$$=\frac{1}{36}$$

$$\text{speed of computers in second group}=\frac{\text{messages}}{\text{computers}\times\text{minutes}}$$
$$=\frac{10}{40\times45}$$
$$=\frac{1}{180}$$

Now we divide these speeds to find how much faster the first group were:
$$\frac{1}{36}\div\frac{1}{180}=5$$

The correct answer is 5 times faster.

10

The length EG is the same as FD.

DFB is a straight line that forms a diagonal across the square $ABCD$.

BF is the radius of the circle.

Let $FD = d$.

Note that the radius of the sector is the same as the side length of the square $ABCD$.

This means $BF = 8$cm

The diagonal across a square forms a right-angled triangle.

We can connect the side lengths using Pythagoras:

$$c^2 = a^2 + b^2$$
$$(d + 8)^2 = 8^2 + 8^2$$
$$(d + 8)(d + 8) = 64 + 64$$
$$d^2 + 8d + 8d + 64 = 128$$
$$d^2 + 16d - 64 = 0$$
$$d = \frac{-16 \pm \sqrt{16^2 - 4(1)(-64)}}{2}$$
$$= \frac{-16 \pm \sqrt{512}}{2}$$
$$= \frac{-16 \pm 16\sqrt{2}}{2}$$
$$= -8 \pm 8\sqrt{2}$$

Expand the brackets.

Collect the terms.

Subtract 128.

Use the quadratic formula:

$$d = \frac{-b \pm \sqrt{b^2 - 4ac}}{2a}$$

Since d is positive only $(-8 + 8\sqrt{2})$ is possible.

d must be positive so the correct answer is $(-8 + 8\sqrt{2})$cm.

Therefore $EG = (-8 + 8\sqrt{2})$cm.

$d = (-8 + 8\sqrt{2})$cm

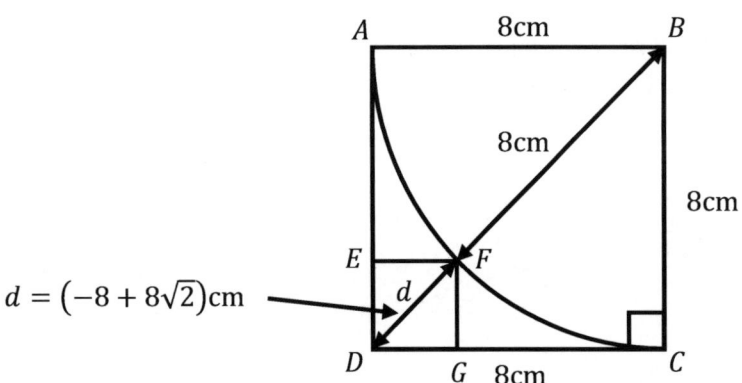
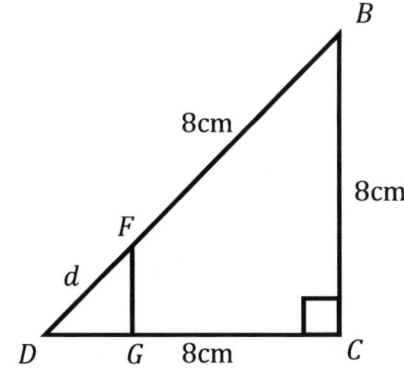

Exercise 7

1

ABC is a straight line that forms a tangent to two circles at A and C.
BE is a straight line that forms a shared tangent to both circles at E.
DE is a diameter of the large circle.
Prove that DA is parallel to EC.

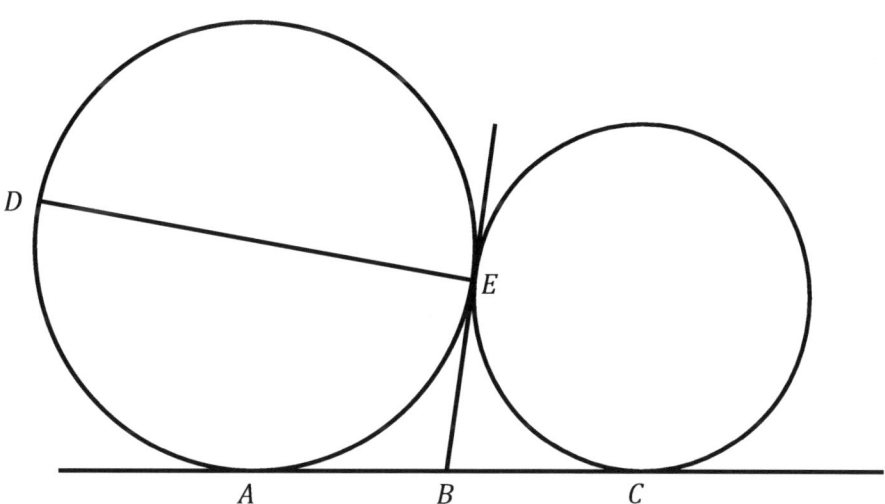

2 calculator

Three marathon runners practise timed laps on a circular track of length 1760 metres.
Runner A has speed 220 metres per minute.
Runner B has speed 330 metres per minute.
Runner C has speed 352 metres per minute.
All three runners start at the same time from the same point.
How many laps will runner C have completed when all three next cross the start line at the same time?

3 calculator

A bag contains red and blue marbles that can be large or small.

red : blue = 5 : 7

large : small = 11 : 4

There are 58 small blue marbles.

Find a possible value for the number of large red marbles.

4 calculator

Tennis rackets are manufactured at a rate of x per hour.

Tennis balls are manufactured at a rate of $(x + 4)$ per hour.

It takes $\frac{5}{4}$ minutes longer to manufacture a tennis racket than a tennis ball.

How many tennis rackets and tennis balls are manufactured in two hours?

5 calculator

Three generators consume 40 litres of fuel in 100 hours.

There are x litres of fuel available for use.

Eight generators operate for 60 hours before two of them break down.

Once a generator breaks down it no longer consumes fuel.

Find the value of x if the remaining generators operate for a further 120 hours.

6

a builders can lay b bricks in c days.

$(a + 4)$ builders can lay $\frac{3}{2}b$ bricks in $\frac{3}{4}c$ days.

Assume that all the builders work at the same rate.

Find the value of a.

7 calculator

In square $ABCD$,

F and E lie on the side AB.

$AE = a$

$FB = 2b$

$AFGH$ is a square that shares two sides with square $ABCD$.

E is the centre of FB.

The shaded area is equal to 192cm^2.

a and b are integers with $a > b$

$a > 4$

$b > 4$

Find the values of a and b.

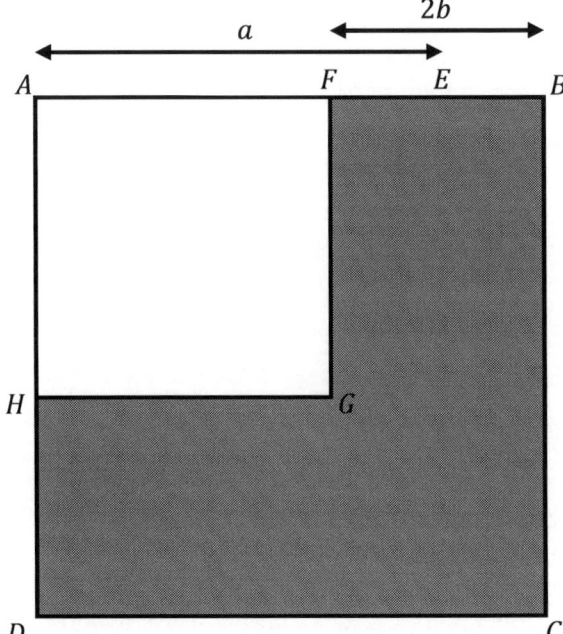

8

$$\frac{A}{B} = \frac{6A}{A + B}$$

Find B as a percentage of A where both A and B are positive.

9 calculator

A square field, $ACIG$, of area 65536m² is to be sold in four lots numbered 1, 2, 3 and 4 at £50/m².
DF and BH are perpendicular straight lines that intersect at point E.
$AB = BE$ and $AD = DE$
$AB : BC = 3 : 1$
The side AB makes an angle of 60° with the line BE as shown.

Find the total amount received for the combined sales of lots 2, 3 and 4, giving your answer to the nearest £100.

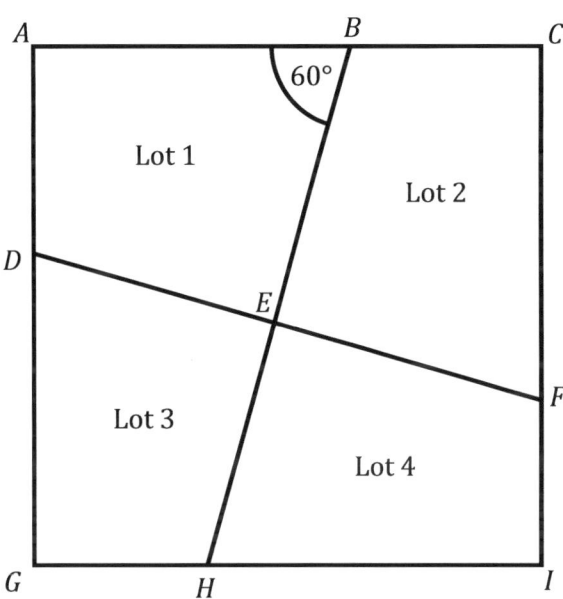

10 calculator

The distance-time graph shows the journey made by a man from home to a bank and back again.
The total distance travelled is 4.8km.
The man travelled to the bank at $v$km/h.
The man spent v minutes in the bank which totalled $\frac{3}{7}$ of the total time.
The man returned home at $\frac{1}{2}v$km/h.
Find the value of v.

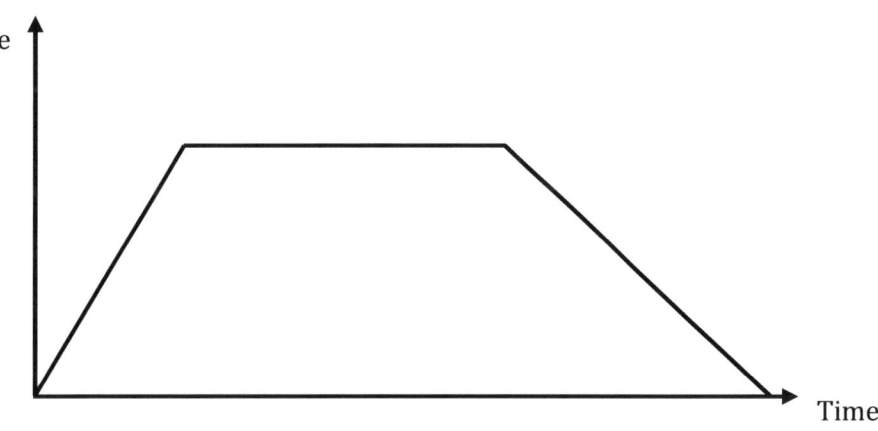

Exercise 7 Solutions

1

Start by joining the sides DA, AE and EC.

Note that $AB = BE$ and $BE = BC$ since tangents drawn from a point to the same circle are equal in length.

This also means that $AB = BC$ so B is the centre of a circle that passes through the points A, E and C.

The angles ADE and EAB are equal by the alternate segment theorem (shown as x).

DE is a diameter which means DE and BE are perpendicular.

Angle $DEB = 90°$

Triangle ABE is isosceles since $AB = BE$

Angle EAB = angle BEA (shown as x).

Triangle BCE is isosceles since $BC = BE$.

angle BCE = angle BEC (shown as y).

Triangle AEC forms a right angle in the semicircle with B as the centre.

Angle $AEC = 90°$ (shown as $x + y$).

Therefore $x + y = 90°$

Angle $DEA = 90° - x$, which is the same as y.

Notice that the angle $DEC = x + 2y$

Notice that angle $ADE = x$

$$\begin{aligned} \text{angle } ADE + \text{angle } DEC &= x + x + 2y \\ &= 2x + 2y \\ &= 2(x + y) \\ &= 2 \times 90° \\ &= 180° \end{aligned}$$

By allied angles, this means that DA is parallel to EC.

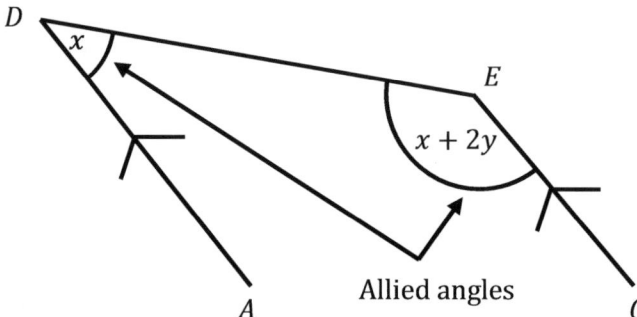

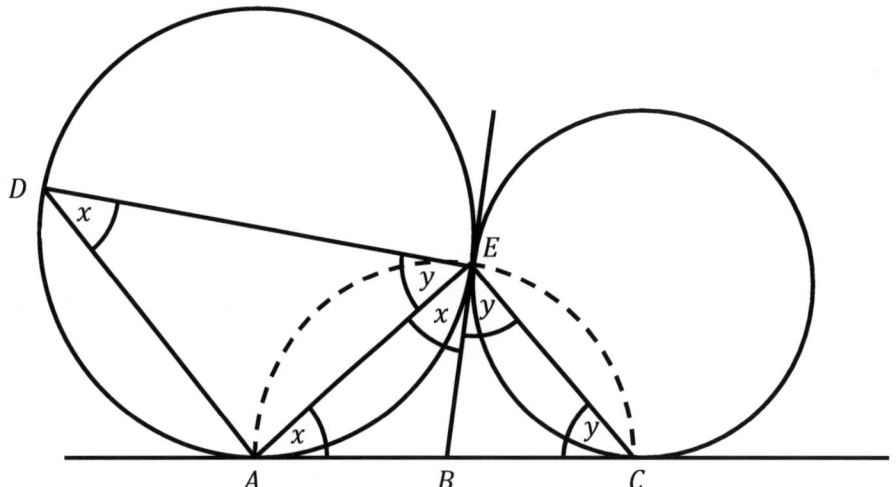

2

This question involves lowest common multiples (LCM).

Questions with multiple events that coincide in time usually involve LCM.

We need to find how long each runner takes to complete a lap:

$$\text{time} = \frac{\text{distance}}{\text{speed}}$$

$$\begin{aligned} \text{runner A time} &= \frac{1760}{220} \\ &= 8 \text{ minutes} \end{aligned}$$

$$\text{runner B time} = \frac{1760}{330}$$
$$= \frac{16}{3} \text{ minutes}$$

$$\text{runner C time} = \frac{1760}{352}$$
$$= 5 \text{ minutes}$$

Now we need to find the LCM for $5, \frac{16}{3}$ and 8.

It is easier to find an LCM if you are dealing with integers.

We can multiply each number by 3, find the LCM, and then divide by 3 to get the required LCM.

We will find the LCM of 15, 16 and 24.

$15 = 3 \times 5$
$16 = 2 \times 2 \times 2 \times 2$
$24 = 2 \times 2 \times 2 \times 3$

With three numbers you can still pair up the factors as you would if you had two numbers.

We can see 2 is shared three times and 3 is shared once.

The LCM is found by multiplying the shared factors once* by the other non-shared factors:

$$\text{LCM} = (\text{shared factors}) \times (\text{non} - \text{shared factors})$$
$$= (2 \times 2 \times 2 \times 3) \times (2 \times 5)$$
$$= 240$$

We now divide by 3 to find the LCM of $5, \frac{16}{3}$ and 8:

$$\frac{240}{3} = 80$$

$$15 = 3 \times 5$$
$$16 = 2 \times 2 \times 2 \times 2$$
$$24 = 2 \times 2 \times 2 \times 3$$

Shared factors circled

The three runners pass the start line together every 80 minutes.

After 80 minutes runner C will have travelled:

$$\text{distance} = \text{speed} \times \text{time}$$
$$= 352 \times 80$$
$$= 28160 \text{ metres}$$

Each lap is 1,760m long so the number of laps completed by runner C will be:

$$\frac{28160}{1760} = 16$$

The correct answer is 16 laps.

*Shared factors can either be shared by just two of the three numbers or by all three of the numbers. Either way they are only included once in the calculation for the LCM.

2 was shared by 16 and 24 three times.

3 was shared by 15 and 24 once.

3

There are two categories for the marbles: large/small or red/blue.

We can construct a two-way table to represent the data.

Call the ratio red : blue $= 5x : 7x$ where x represents the multiplier that gives the true values.

Call the ratio large : small $= 11y : 4y$ where y represents the multiplier that gives the true values.

	Small	Large	
Red			$5x$
Blue	58		$7x$
	$4y$	$11y$	

The totals $11y + 4y = 15y$ and $5x + 7x = 12x$ each refer to the total number of marbles.
The number of marbles must be an integer.
Since this integer can be divided into 15 and 12, it must be a multiple of both 15 and 12.
Now we can draw another two-way table, only this time we will write each space in terms of the total number of marbles, which we will call n.

	Small	Large	
Red	$\frac{4}{15}n - 58$	$\frac{5}{12}n - \left(\frac{4}{15}n - 58\right)$	$\frac{5}{12}n$
Blue	58		$\frac{7}{12}n$
	$\frac{4}{15}n$	$\frac{11}{15}n$	n

Note that if 58 are small blue, and there are $\frac{4}{15}n$ small marbles in total, then $\frac{4}{15}n - 58$ will represent the number of small red marbles.

If $\frac{5}{12}n$ represents the number of red marbles and $\frac{4}{15}n - 58$ are small red marbles then $\frac{5}{12}n - \left(\frac{4}{15}n - 58\right)$ must represent the number of large red marbles.

We can simplify the expression for the number of large red marbles:

$$\frac{5}{12}n - \left(\frac{4}{15}n - 58\right) = \frac{5}{12}n - \frac{4}{15}n + 58$$
$$= \frac{3}{20}n + 58$$

There are an infinite number of answers to the question because we are identifying an integer that can be divided by 15 and 12.

For the expression $\frac{3}{20}n + 58$, we need to substitute a value of n that would produce an integer answer.

The value must be at least 20, otherwise $\frac{3}{20}n$ will remain a fraction.

We already know that n must be at least 60 because this is the lowest common multiple of 12 and 15.
We know that any entry in the two-way table must be a positive integer.
We can use an inequality to speed up the search for a value of n.
We can use the expression for the number of small red marbles, which must be greater than zero:

$$\frac{4}{15}n - 58 > 0$$
$$\frac{4}{15}n > 58$$
$$4n > 870$$
$$n > 217.5$$

	Small	Large	
Red	6	94	100
Blue	58	82	140
	64	176	240

The most immediate multiple of 60 above 217.5 is 240.
Try $n = 240$,

$$\frac{3}{20}(240) + 58 = 36 + 58$$
$$= 94$$

One possible answer is 94 (shown in the completed table).

We know each possible value of n must be the multiples of 60 from 240 onwards: 300, 360, 420, etc.
So other possible answers are 103, 112, 121 ...
In general, any answer of the form $9x + 94$ where $x \geq 0$ will be acceptable.

4

The link given between the two manufacturing rates is given as a time.
This means we need each manufacturing rate given as a time to manufacture in minutes.
Tennis rackets are manufactured at a rate of x per hour.
This means it takes $\frac{60}{x}$ minutes to manufacture one tennis racket.
Tennis balls are manufactured at a rate of $(x + 4)$ per hour.
This means it takes $\frac{60}{x+4}$ minutes to manufacture one tennis ball.
We know it takes $\frac{5}{4}$ minutes longer to manufacture a tennis racket so we can form and solve an equation for x.

tennis racket time = tennis ball time $+ \dfrac{5}{4}$

$$\frac{60}{x} = \frac{60}{x+4} + \frac{5}{4}$$

$$60 = \frac{60x}{x+4} + \frac{5x}{4} \qquad \text{Multiply by } x.$$

$$60(x+4) = 60x + \frac{5x(x+4)}{4} \qquad \text{Multiply by } (x+4).$$

$$240(x+4) = 240x + 5x(x+4) \qquad \text{Multiply by 4.}$$

$$240x + 960 = 240x + 5x^2 + 20x \qquad \text{Expand the brackets.}$$

$$5x^2 + 20x - 960 = 0 \qquad \text{Simplify the quadratic and set the equation equal to zero.}$$

$$x^2 + 4x - 192 = 0 \qquad \text{Factorise.}$$

$$(x + 16)(x - 12) = 0 \qquad \text{Reject the negative solution.}$$

$x = 12$ is the correct solution since x must be positive.
In two hours $2(12) = 24$ tennis rackets are manufactured.
In two hours $2(12 + 4) = 32$ tennis balls are manufactured.

5

This is a variation question.
The variables are generators, fuel and time in hours.
We must clarify how the variables are related.
Generators are proportional to fuel: more generators need more fuel.
Generators are inversely proportional to time: more generators consume the same fuel in less time.
Fuel is directly proportional to time: more fuel means the generators operate for longer.
We can represent the variables in a table.

Generators	Fuel	Hours	
3	40	100	Start with the input values.
8	$\dfrac{320}{3}$	100	Generators and fuel both multiplied by $\dfrac{8}{3}$.
8	64	60	Fuel and hours both multiplied by $\dfrac{60}{100}$.

There were x litres of fuel available but 64L have been used.
There will now be $(x - 64)$ litres available for the remaining 6 generators.

Generators	Fuel	Hours	
3	40	100	Start with the input values.
6	80	100	Generators and fuel both multiplied by 2.
6	96	120	Fuel and hours both multiplied by $\frac{120}{100}$.

So the remaining generators consume 96L of fuel.
We know that this is equal to $(x - 64)$ litres:
$x - 64 = 96$
$\qquad x = 160$

The correct answer is 160L of fuel were available for use.

6

This is a variation question.
The variables are builders, bricks and time in days.
We must clarify how the variables are related.
Builders are proportional to bricks: more builders lay more bricks.
Builders are inversely proportional to time: more builders lay bricks in less time.
Bricks are directly proportional to time: more bricks take longer to lay.
We can represent the variables in a table.

Builders	Bricks	Days	
a	b	c	Start with the input values.
$\frac{3}{2}a$	$\frac{3}{2}b$	c	Builders and bricks both multiplied by $\frac{3}{2}$.
$2a$	$\frac{3}{2}b$	$\frac{3}{4}c$	Days multiplied by $\frac{3}{4}$. Builders multiplied by $\frac{4}{3}$ (inverse proportion).

However, we already know that $(a + 4)$ builders can lay $\frac{3}{2}b$ bricks in $\frac{3}{4}c$ days.
The table shows this to be equivalent to $2a$, so we can form and solve an equation for a:
$2a = a + 4$
$\qquad a = 4$

The correct answer is 4.

7

If E is the centre of FB then $FE = EB$.
We can say $EB = b$ and $FE = b$.
The length of AB is $(a + b)$.
The length of AF is $(a - b)$.
Note side AHD will mirror side AFB.
This allows us to form an equation for the shaded area.
shaded area $= (a + b)^2 - (a - b)^2$

This expression is the difference of two squares (the squares themselves are expressions).

$$(a + b)^2 - (a - b)^2 = (a + b + (a - b))(a + b - (a - b))$$
$$= (a + b + a - b)(a + b - a + b)$$
$$= 2a \times 2b$$
$$= 4ab$$

We know that the shaded area is 192cm^2 so we can write:
$$4ab = 192$$
$$ab = 48$$

Since both a and b are greater than 4, the only factor pair of 48 that meets this requirement is 8×6
The correct answer is $a = 8$ and $b = 6$.

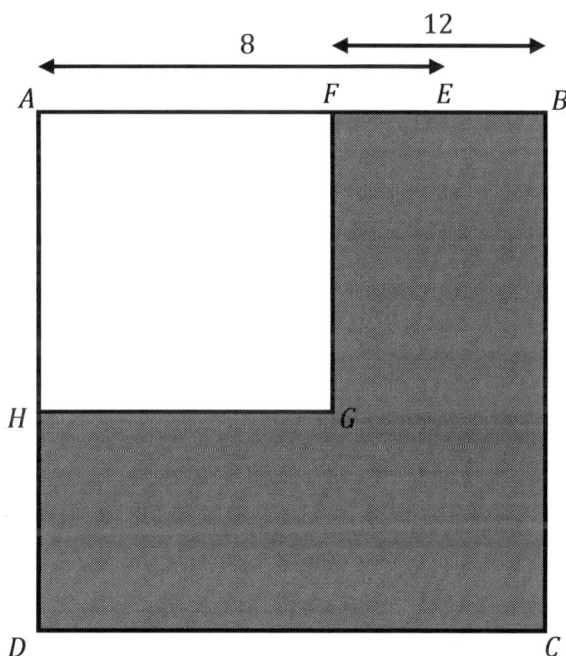

8

To find B as a percentage of A we need to rearrange the equation to form $\frac{B}{A}$ and obtain a numerical value that it is equal to:

$$\frac{A}{B} = \frac{6A}{A + B}$$
$$\frac{1}{B} = \frac{6}{A + B} \qquad \text{Divide by } A.$$
$$\frac{A + B}{B} = 6 \qquad \text{Multiply by } (A + B).$$
$$A + B = 6B \qquad \text{Multiply by } B.$$
$$A = 5B \qquad \text{Subtract } B.$$
$$\frac{A}{5} = B \qquad \text{Divide by 5.}$$
$$\frac{1}{5} = \frac{B}{A} \qquad \text{Divide by } A.$$
$$\frac{1}{5} = 20\%$$

Therefore B as a percentage of A is 20%.

9

We are given the area of the whole field as 65536m².
Since the field is a square we can find the side length of the field:

$$AC = \sqrt{65536}$$
$$= 256$$

The side AC is divided into the ratio $AB : BC = 3 : 1$

$$AB = \frac{3}{4} \times 256$$
$$= 192$$

If $AB = BE$ and $AD = DE$, then the quadrilateral $ABED$ is a kite.
We know that the angles DAB and BED are both 90°.
The angle $ADE = 120°$ as there are 360° in a quadrilateral.
We can split the kite $ABED$ in half along the line DB.
Then we can find the area of triangle ABD using the
side lengths AB and AD.
We know $AB = 192$m so we need AD.
Using trigonometry SOHCAHTOA we obtain:

$$\tan 30° = \frac{\text{opposite}}{\text{adjacent}}$$
$$= \frac{AD}{AB}$$
$$= \frac{AD}{192}$$
$$AD = 192 \tan 30°$$
$$= \frac{192}{\sqrt{3}}$$

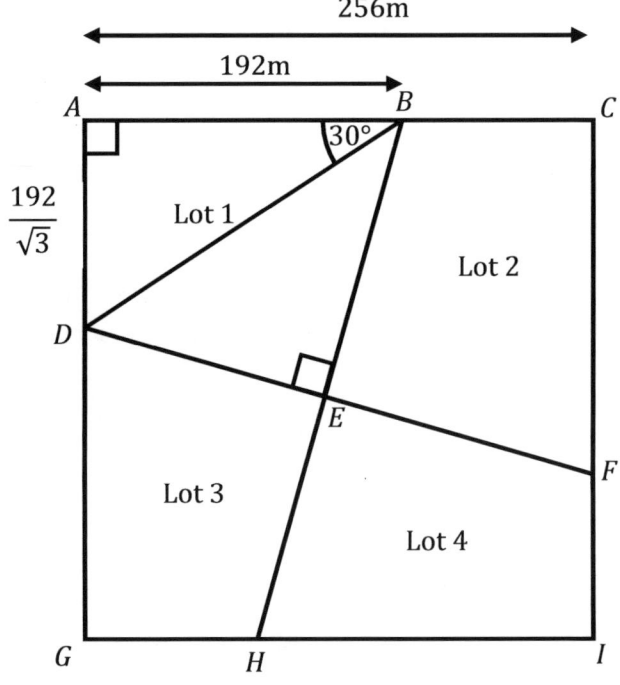

The area of the triangle ABD can be doubled to
find the area of the kite $ABED$:
area of kite $ABED$ = 2 × area of triangle ABD

$$= 2 \times \frac{1}{2} \times 192 \times \frac{192}{\sqrt{3}}$$
$$= \frac{36864}{\sqrt{3}}$$

The cost of the whole field $ACIG$ will be: $65536 \times 50 = £3276800$
The cost of lot 1 will be: $\frac{36864}{\sqrt{3}} \times 50 = £1064172.02$
The difference in cost will be the cost of lots 2,3 and 4.
cost of lots 2, 3 and 4 = £3276800 − £1064172.02
$$= £2212627.98$$

The answer to the nearest £100 is £2212600.

10

The gradient of a distance-time graph is the speed.
The first part of the journey was at speed v, so the gradient here is v.
The third part of the journey was at speed $\frac{1}{2}v$, so the gradient here is $\frac{1}{2}v$ (ignoring the negative).
The man travelled the same distance to and from the bank.
Since the speed had a ratio to bank : from bank = 2 : 1, we know that the return journey took twice as long

as the outward journey.

Let the time taken to get to the bank be x hours; then the time taken to return from the bank will be $2x$ hours.

The total journey distance is 4.8km so the journey to the bank would be 2.4km.

We can now form an equation involving x and v.

From the first part of the journey:

$$\text{speed} = \frac{\text{distance}}{\text{time}}$$
$$v = \frac{2.4}{x}$$
$$vx = 2.4 \quad [1]$$

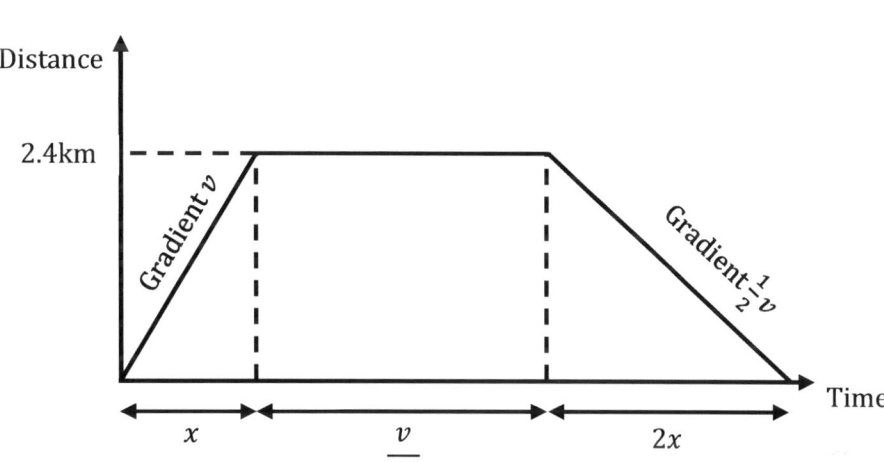

We also know that the middle part of the journey was v minutes.

Note that this would be $\frac{v}{60}$ hours.

This makes the time consistent with the x unit introduced earlier.

The total journey time is:

$$x + \frac{v}{60} + 2x = 3x + \frac{v}{60}$$

We know that $\frac{v}{60}$ represents $\frac{3}{7}$ of the total journey time.

We can form and simplify another equation:

$$\frac{v}{60} = \frac{3}{7}\left(3x + \frac{v}{60}\right)$$
$$\frac{7v}{60} = 3\left(3x + \frac{v}{60}\right) \qquad \text{Multiply by 7.}$$
$$7v = 180\left(3x + \frac{v}{60}\right) \qquad \text{Multiply by 60.}$$
$$= 540x + 3v \qquad \text{Expand the brackets.}$$
$$4v = 540x \qquad \text{Subtract } 3v.$$
$$v = 135x \qquad \text{Divide by 4.}$$
$$x = \frac{v}{135} \quad [2] \qquad \text{Divide by 135.}$$

We can substitute equation [2] into [1] and eliminate x to find v.

$$vx = 2.4$$
$$v\left(\frac{v}{135}\right) = 2.4 \qquad \text{Substitute } x = \frac{v}{135} \text{ into equation [1].}$$
$$\qquad\qquad\qquad \text{Expand the brackets.}$$
$$\frac{v^2}{135} = 2.4$$
$$v^2 = 324 \qquad \text{Multiply by 135.}$$
$$\qquad\qquad\qquad \text{Square root.}$$
$$v = 18$$

The correct answer is $v = 18$km/h or 18 minutes.

Exercise 8

1

The circle shown has radius r cm.
ADB is a chord in the circle.
The chord has length $2c$ cm.
The line CD bisects the chord ADB and has length h cm.
$h : c = 2 : 5$
Find r in terms of h.

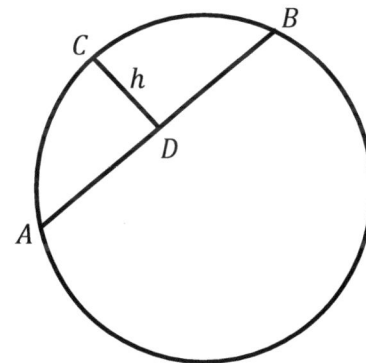

2 calculator

$ABCD$ is a parallelogram.
AC and BD are the two diagonals of the parallelogram and they meet at point E.
$AD = 5$ cm, $AE = 3.4$ cm and $DE = 4.2$ cm.
Find the area of the parallelogram.

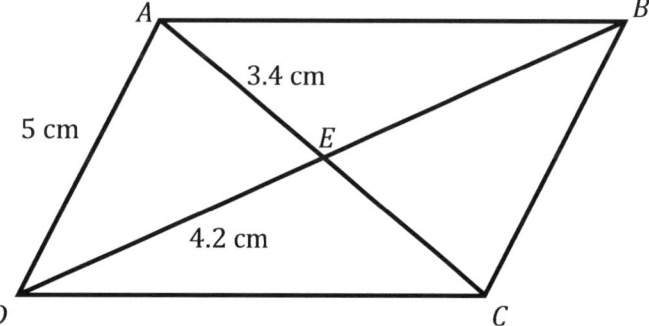

3

A train journey has a distance of 75 miles.
When the average speed of the train is reduced by 10mph the journey takes 5 minutes longer to complete.
Find the normal speed of the train.

4 calculator

OX is a vertical line which cuts the circle shown at Q and R.
OY is a horizontal line that forms a tangent to the circle
at the point P.
The circle has a radius of 17cm.
QR has length 16cm.
Find the area of the segment shown as the shaded
region in the diagram.

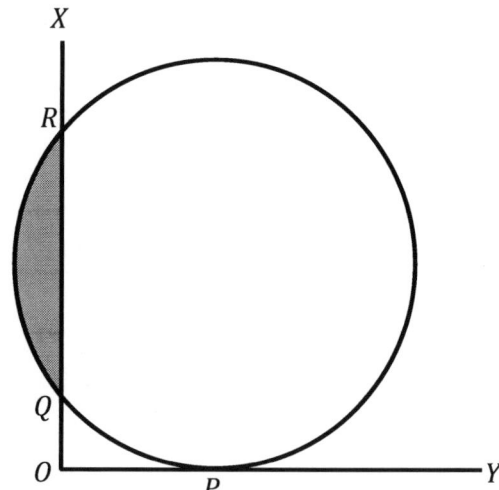

5

A circle is drawn inside the triangle ABC with each of the sides of ABC forming tangents to the circle at the points P, Q and R.
Another triangle is drawn inside the circle with vertices at the points P, Q and R.
Angle $PQR = 50°$.
Angle $QRP = 62°$.
Angle $RPQ = 68°$.
Find the three angles of the triangle ABC.

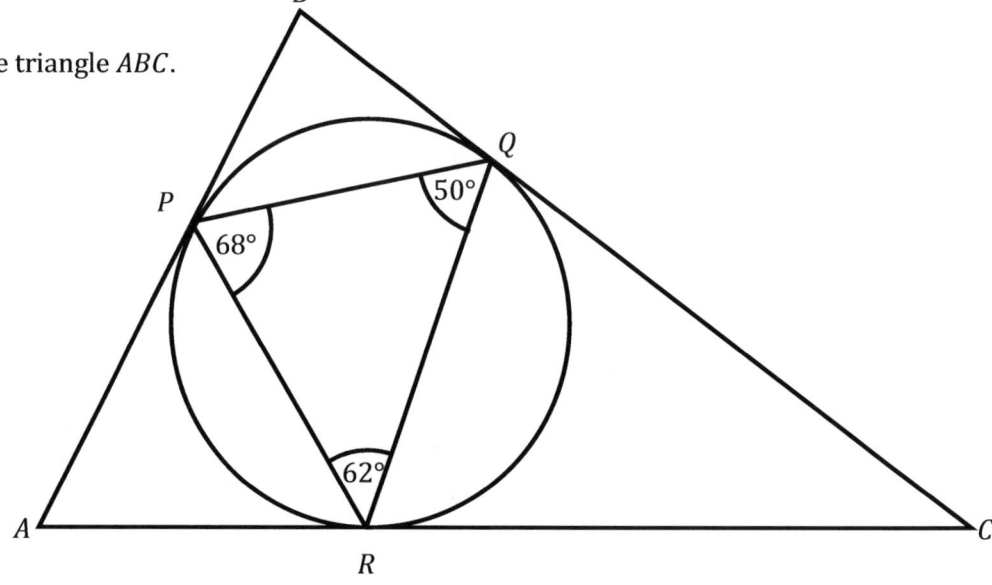

6

A temperature gauge is suspected to be inaccurate.
When the temperature gauge shows a value of 16°C the real temperature is 18°C.
When the temperature gauge shows a value of 32°C the real temperature is 30°C.
The real temperature is thought to be related to the temperature shown on the gauge by an equation of the form $a + bt$.
a and b are constants.
t is the temperature value shown on the gauge.
Find what temperature the gauge will show when the real temperature is 0°C.

7

The equilateral triangle ABC is enlarged by scale factor $-\frac{5}{2}$ about the origin to form triangle DEF.
The point A has coordinates $(a-4, b)$ and point C has coordinates (a, b).
Find the coordinates of E in terms of a and b, giving your answer in surd form.

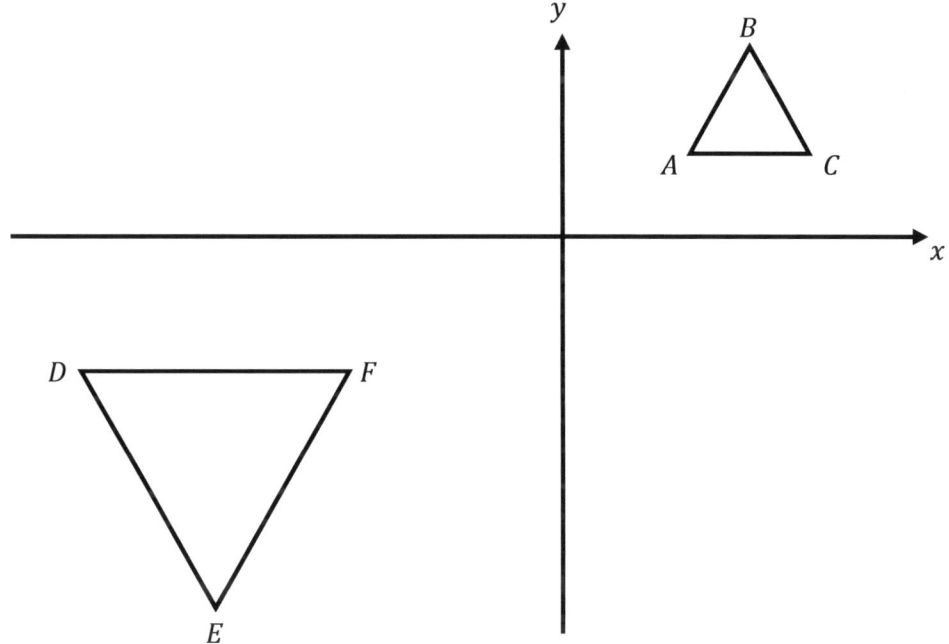

8

The nth term of sequence A is defined by $2n^2 - 4n + 3$
The nth term of sequence B is defined by $n^2 - 2n + 3$

Show using algebra that the terms of sequence A are all greater than those of sequence B for all $n > 2$

9

a and b are positive integers greater than 1.
Prove that $\left(a^b - 1\right)$ is a factor of $\left(a^{4b} - 1\right)$.

10 calculator

One chicken consumes one kilogram of food in 24 hours.
There are 21kg of food available to eat.
Two groups of chickens are each given 21kg of food.

In the first group,
x chickens consume food for 6 hours followed by $(x-4)$ chickens until the food is gone.

In the second group,
$(x-4)$ chickens consume food for 6 hours followed by x chickens until the food is gone.

It is found that the second group finishes all the food in 2 hours less than the first group.
Find the value of x.

Exercise 8 Solutions

1

If the line CD bisects the chord ADB then CD must be perpendicular to ADB.
The chord has length $2c$ so $AD = c$ and $DB = c$.
We need to find an equation connecting r, c and h.
We can do this using Pythagoras: $a^2 + b^2 = c^2$.
Let the centre of the circle be O.
We can say that the length $OD = r - h$.
The length $OA = r$.
This completes the sides of the right-angled triangle OAD.

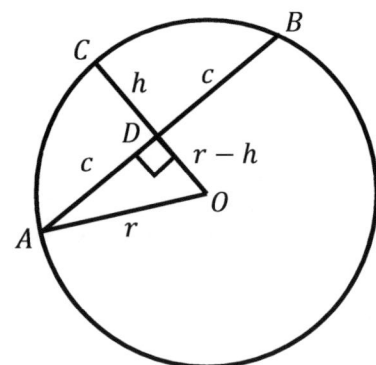

Using Pythagoras:
$$OD^2 + AD^2 = OA^2$$
$$(r - h)^2 + c^2 = r^2$$

$(r - h)(r - h) + c^2 = r^2$ Expand the brackets.

$r^2 - rh - rh + h^2 + c^2 = r^2$ Collect the terms.

$h^2 + c^2 - 2rh = 0$ [1]   Cancel the r^2 from both sides.

Now we need to replace c in terms of h.
We do this using ratio cross multiplication:
$h : c = 2 : 5$ can be written as $2c = 5h$.

Making c the subject we obtain $c = \frac{5}{2}h$.

Substituting this into equation [1]:

Cross multiplying a ratio

$h : c$

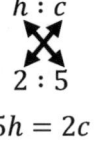

$2 : 5$

$5h = 2c$

$h^2 + \left(\frac{5}{2}h\right)^2 - 2rh = 0$ Replace c^2 with $\left(\frac{5}{2}h\right)^2$.

$h^2 + \frac{25}{4}h^2 - 2rh = 0$ $\left(\frac{5}{2}h\right)^2 = \frac{25}{4}h^2$.

$\frac{29}{4}h^2 - 2rh = 0$ Collect the h^2 terms.

$\frac{29}{4}h - 2r = 0$ Divide by h (h is never zero).

$2r = \frac{29}{4}h$ Add $2r$.

$r = \frac{29}{8}h$ Divide by 2.

The correct answer is $r = \frac{29}{8}h$.

2

In a parallelogram the diagonals bisect each other.
This means that $AE = EC$ and $DE = EB$.
The proof of this is to show that the triangles ADE and BCE are congruent.
If $AD = 5$cm then $BC = 5$cm since opposite sides are equal in length in a parallelogram.
Angle DAC is equal to angle ACB because they are alternate angles.
Angle ADB is equal to angle DBC because they are alternate angles.
This means we have angle-side-angle equal in triangles ADE and BCE, so they are congruent.
The side AE is between angles DAC and AED.
The side EC is between angles ACB and BEC.
Since these pairs of angles are equal to each other and we have congruent triangles we can say that the sides AE and EC are equal.
This means that sides DE and EB will also be equal as they make up the third side in the congruent

triangles.

By an identical argument we can say that triangles AEB and DEC are also congruent.

Congruent triangles have the same area.

The angles described earlier are denoted by x, y and z in the diagram.

The angles shown by x are alternate.
The angles shown by y are alternate.
The angles shown by z are opposite.

The white triangles are congruent.
The shaded triangles are congruent.
All four triangles have equal area.

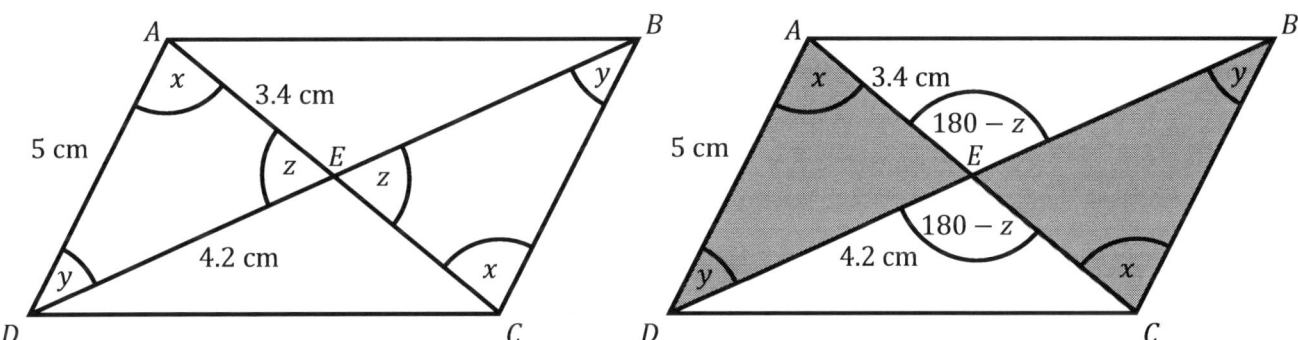

To calculate the area of a triangle we use the sine area formula: $\frac{1}{2}ab\sin C$.

You need an angle sandwiched between two sides for this formula.

At present we do not know any angles so we would need to use the cosine rule to get one.

The angle we choose is angle z.

The reason for this is that angle z is on the straight line DEB.

The supplementary angle to z can be written as $(180 - z)$.

Supplementary means the angles sum to $180°$.

This is significant when using the sine area formula.

If you type $\sin 30°$ in the calculator you get $\frac{1}{2}$.

If you type $\sin 150°$ in the calculator you get $\frac{1}{2}$.

In fact if you type any such pairing of sine values, $\sin x$ and then $\sin(180 - x)$, you will generate the same answer.

If we had to apply the sine area formula $\left(\frac{1}{2}ab\sin C\right)$ to two triangles where the only difference between them was the angle we chose for C, both triangles have the same area when the angles are z and $(180 - z)$

For the parallelogram in question, we will need to calculate the area of triangle AED:

area of triangle $AED = \frac{1}{2} \times 4.2 \times 3.4 \times \sin z$

and the area of triangle AEB:

area of triangle $AEB = \frac{1}{2} \times 4.2 \times 3.4 \times \sin(180 - z)$

As stated previously, the sine of the angles z and $180 - z$ will be equal.

This means that triangles AED and AEB are equal in area.

Because we also know triangle AED is congruent to triangle BEC and triangle AEB is congruent to triangle DEC, we can say that all four of the triangles in a parallelogram have the same area.

Now we can use the cosine rule to find the angle z:

$$a^2 = b^2 + c^2 - 2bc \cos A$$
$$AD^2 = AE^2 + DE^2 - 2(AE)(DE) \cos z$$
$$5^2 = 3.4^2 + 4.2^2 - 2(3.4)(4.2) \cos z$$
$$25 = 29.2 - 28.56 \cos z$$
$$-4.2 = -28.56 \cos z$$
$$\cos z = \frac{4.2}{28.56}$$
$$= 0.147 \ldots$$
$$z = \cos^{-1} 0.147 \ldots$$
$$= 81.5 \ldots °$$

And now the sine area formula for triangle AED.
Note that we will also multiply this by 4 to get the area of the parallelogram:

$$\text{area of parallelogram} = 4 \times \frac{1}{2} ab \sin C$$
$$= 2(AE)(DE) \sin z$$
$$= 2(3.4)(4.2) \sin 81.5 \ldots °$$
$$= 28.249 \ldots$$

The area of the parallelogram is 28.2cm^2 correct to three significant figures.

3

Call the time the train normally takes t hours.
The normal speed of the train will be:

$$\text{speed} = \frac{\text{distance}}{\text{time}}$$
$$= \frac{75}{t}$$

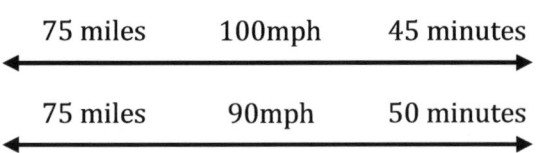

The speed is now reduced by 10mph:

$$\text{new speed} = \frac{75}{t} - 10$$

The journey now takes 5 minutes longer.
For consistency we must divide this time by 60 to convert to hours: $\frac{5}{60}$.

$$\text{new time} = t + \frac{5}{60}$$
$$= t + \frac{1}{12}$$

The distance is still 75 miles so we can form an equation:

distance = new speed × new time

$$75 = \left(\frac{75}{t} - 10\right) \times \left(t + \frac{1}{12}\right)$$
Write each term over a common denominator.

$$= \frac{75 - 10t}{t} \times \frac{12t + 1}{12}$$
Multiply the numerators and denominators together.

$$= \frac{(75 - 10t)(12t + 1)}{12t}$$
Multiply by $12t$.

$$900t = (75 - 10t)(12t + 1)$$
Multiply out the brackets.

$$900t = 900t + 75 - 120t^2 - 10t$$
Cancel the $900t$ from both sides.

$$120t^2 + 10t - 75 = 0$$
Rearrange the quadratic and set equal to zero.

$24t^2 + 2t - 15 = 0$ Divide by 5.

$(6t + 5)(4t - 3) = 0$ Factorise the quadratic.

$t = \frac{3}{4}$ is the only valid solution.   Reject the negative solution.

We can calculate the normal speed of the train:

$$\text{speed} = \frac{\text{distance}}{\text{time}}$$
$$= \frac{75}{t}$$
$$= \frac{75}{\frac{3}{4}}$$
$$= 100$$

The normal speed of the train is 100mph.

4

Call the centre of the circle T.

The shaded area forms a segment.

To find the area of the segment we require the area of sector TRQ and triangle TRQ.

The area of the segment is given by:

area of segment = area of sector TRQ − area of triangle TRQ

The area of a sector is found using the formula:

$$\text{area of sector} = \frac{\text{angle of sector}}{360} \times \pi r^2$$

The area of the triangle can be found using the sine area formula: $\frac{1}{2}ab\sin C$.

a and b are equal to the radius of the circle (17cm) and angle C is the same as the angle of the sector.

We can bisect (split in half) the chord RQ by drawing a line from T towards the circumference.

Call the point where the chord is split S.

We can then draw a line TQ which will be equal to the radius (17cm).

The side length SQ will be 8cm (half the chord).

We can now use Pythagoras to link the sides TQ, TS and SQ together.

$$a^2 + b^2 = c^2$$
$$TS^2 + SQ^2 = TQ^2$$
$$TS^2 + 8^2 = 17^2$$
$$TS^2 + 64 = 289$$
$$TS^2 = 225$$
$$TS = 15$$

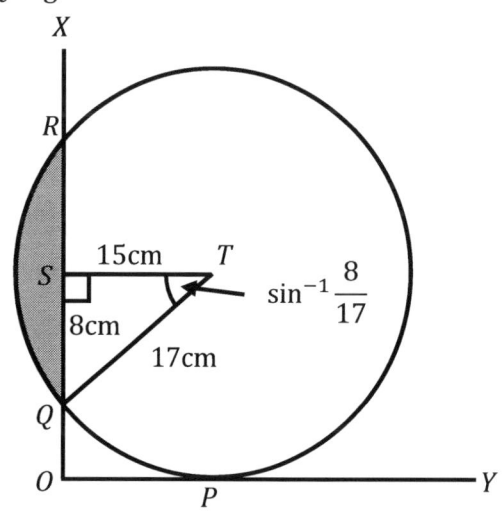

We now need the angle RTQ.

We can get this angle by doubling the angle STQ

Angle STQ is found using trigonometry SOHCAHTOA.

$$\sin(STQ) = \frac{\text{opposite}}{\text{hypotenuse}}$$
$$= \frac{8}{17}$$

Angle $STQ = \sin^{-1}\frac{8}{17}$

We can leave this in exact form.

This means angle $RTQ = 2\sin^{-1}\frac{8}{17}$

We can now use the formula described above for the area of the segment:
area of segment = area of sector TRQ − area of triangle TRQ

$$= \frac{2\sin^{-1}\frac{8}{17}}{360} \times \pi \times 17^2 - \frac{1}{2} \times 17 \times 17 \times \sin\left(2\sin^{-1}\frac{8}{17}\right)$$
$$= 21.597\ldots$$

The answer is 21.6cm^2 correct to three significant figures.

5

Let the centre of the circle be O.
We can form 3 quadrilaterals, $APOR, CROQ$ and $BPOQ$.
Each quadrilateral will be a kite because they each have two pairs of equal-length sides.
Two tangents drawn from a point are equal in length.
This means $AP = AR, CR = CQ$ and $BP = BQ$.
All the other sides in the kites, OP, OQ and OR are all radii so will be the same length.
A tangent to a radius always forms a right angle.
Each of the three kites will have two right angles in them.
Since the interior angles of a quadrilateral sum to 360° (with 180° accounted for by the right angles) we know the other two angles sum to 180°.
We can find the angles POR, ROQ and POQ using the circle theorem "angle at centre equals twice angle at the circumference".

Angle $POR = 2 \times 50$
$\qquad\quad = 100°$
Angle $ROQ = 2 \times 68$
$\qquad\quad = 136°$
Angle $POQ = 2 \times 62$
$\qquad\quad = 124°$

Now we can find the three angles of the triangle ABC:
Angle $BAC = 180 - 100$
$\qquad\quad = 80°$
Angle $ACB = 180 - 136$
$\qquad\quad = 44°$
Angle $ABC = 180 - 124$
$\qquad\quad = 56°$

The correct angles are 44°, 56° and 80°.

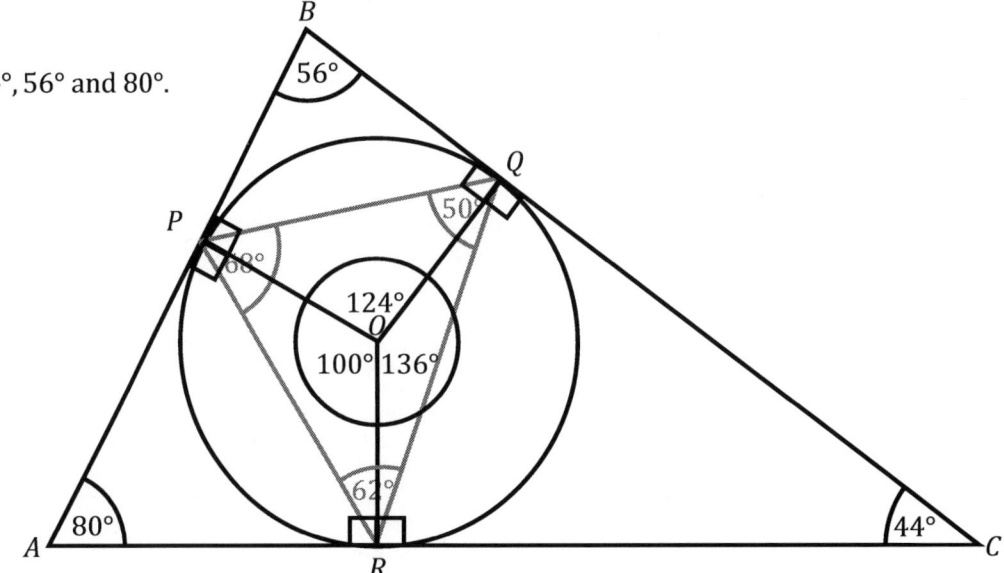

Angle at centre is twice the
angle at the circumference

6

Note that the equation $a + bt$ is a linear equation with t the temperature shown on the gauge.
We have two pairs of values that are linked by $a + bt$.
Call the real temperature v.
Then we can say $v = a + bt$ which would read as:
real temperature $= a + b \times$ gauge temperature

We know $v = 18$ when $t = 16$ and $v = 30$ when $t = 32$.
This forms the basis for two simultaneous equations that we can use to solve for a and b.
$$a + b \times 16 = 18$$
$$a + 16b = 18 \quad [1]$$
$$a + b \times 32 = 30$$
$$a + 32b = 30 \quad [2]$$

We can now subtract equation [1] from equation [2] to obtain:
$$16b = 12$$
$$b = \frac{12}{16}$$
$$= \frac{3}{4}$$

$$\begin{aligned} a + 32b &= 30 \quad [2] \\ - \quad a + 16b &= 18 \quad [1] \\ \hline 16b &= 12 \\ b &= \frac{3}{4} \end{aligned}$$

Now we substitute $b = \frac{3}{4}$ into equation [1]:
$$a + 16b = 18$$
$$a + 16\left(\frac{3}{4}\right) = 18$$
$$a + 12 = 18$$
$$a = 6$$

The full equation is $v = 6 + \frac{3}{4}t$.
Now we can find what temperature the gauge will show when the real temperature is $0°C$ ($v = 0$).

$$v = 6 + \frac{3}{4}t$$
$$0 = 6 + \frac{3}{4}t \qquad \text{Substitute } v = 0 \text{ into the equation.}$$
$$-6 = \frac{3}{4}t \qquad \text{Subtract 6.}$$
$$-24 = 3t \qquad \text{Multiply by 4.}$$
$$-8 = t \qquad \text{Divide by 3.}$$

The gauge would show a
temperature of $-8°C$ when
the real temperature was $0°C$.
The graph shows the linear
relationship $v = 6 + \frac{3}{4}t$.

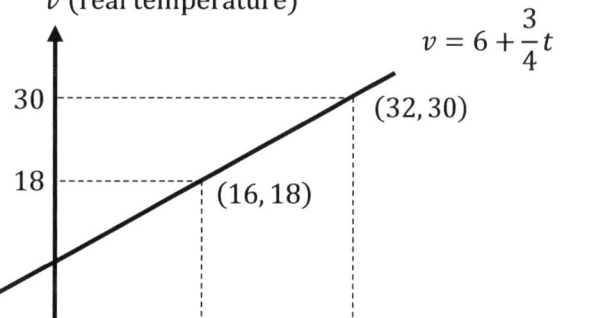

91

7

An enlargement can be thought of as a multiplier applied to each coordinate of the shape being enlarged.
Normally the coordinates of the shape are in the form (x, y) defined by the origin.
The coordinates of the shape being enlarged are defined in terms of the centre of enlargement.
For example,
A shape may have a point with coordinates $(4, 3)$ which will be transformed under an enlargement of scale factor 2 with centre of enlargement $(1, 1)$.
The position of the coordinates $(4, 3)$ relative to the centre of enlargement $(1, 1)$ is $(3, 2)$.
The $(3, 2)$ is really describing a vector $\begin{pmatrix} 3 \\ 2 \end{pmatrix}$.
It is this vector that we apply the scale factor to:
$$2\begin{pmatrix} 3 \\ 2 \end{pmatrix} = \begin{pmatrix} 6 \\ 4 \end{pmatrix}$$

This vector is then applied to the centre of enlargement $(1, 1)$ to give the new coordinates of $(4, 3)$.
So the new location of the coordinates $(4, 3)$ would be $(7, 5)$.
The diagram below shows this example.

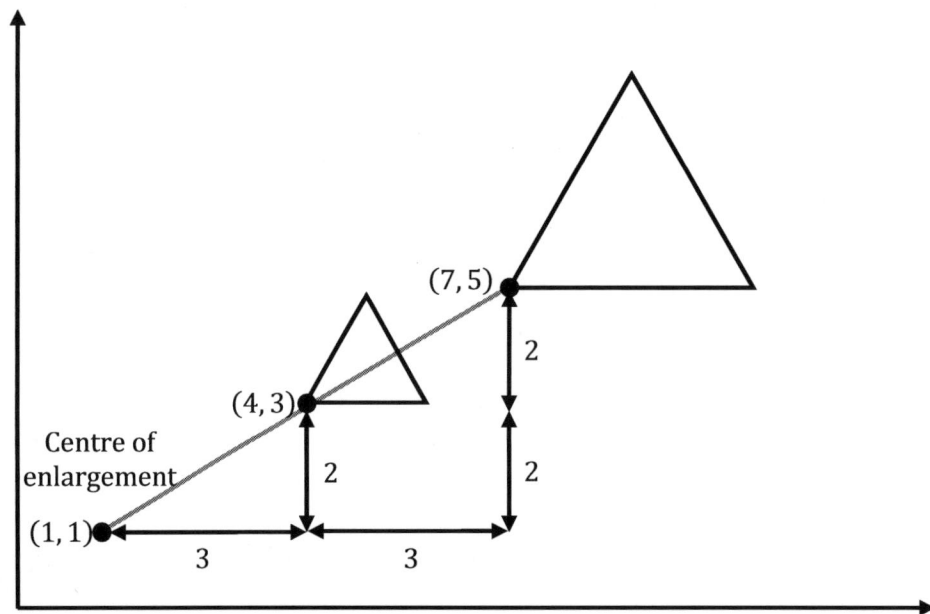

With this question the centre of enlargement is the origin, so any coordinates on the triangle ABC can be considered as a vector describing their location relative to the centre of enlargement.
The coordinates of the point B are not explicitly stated; they will be in terms of a and b.
We need to determine the coordinates of B in terms of a and b because B is mapped to the point E under the given transformation.
We use the properties of an equilateral triangle to do this.

Notice that the x coordinate of A is $(a - 4)$ and that of C is a.
Both A and C are on the same horizontal line since their y-coordinates are both b.
This means that the x-direction determines the side length AC.
The difference between $a - 4$ and a is 4.
So we know the triangle ABC has side length 4.

We know that point B will be directly above the middle of the line AC so the x-coordinate of B is $a - 2$.
To get the y-coordinate of B we need to split the triangle ABC in half and use Pythagoras.
Call the point where the line from B meets AC, X.

We can then write:
$$BX^2 + XC^2 = BC^2$$
$$BX^2 + 2^2 = 4^2$$
$$BX^2 + 4 = 16$$
$$BX^2 = 12$$
$$BX = 2\sqrt{3}$$

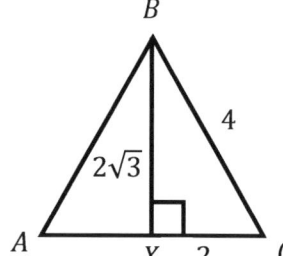

This means the y-coordinate of B will be $b + 2\sqrt{3}$.
The coordinates of B are $\left(a - 2, b + 2\sqrt{3}\right)$.

We can now apply the scale factor $-\frac{5}{2}$ to the coordinates of B to find the coordinates of E.

We can think of the coordinates of B as a column vector: $\begin{pmatrix} a - 2 \\ b + 2\sqrt{3} \end{pmatrix}$

Now we apply the scale factor to this column vector:

$$-\frac{5}{2}\begin{pmatrix} a - 2 \\ b + 2\sqrt{3} \end{pmatrix} = \begin{pmatrix} -\frac{5}{2}(a - 2) \\ -\frac{5}{2}(b + 2\sqrt{3}) \end{pmatrix}$$

This new column vector will be the coordinates of point E.
The correct answer is $\left(-\frac{5}{2}(a - 2), -\frac{5}{2}(b + 2\sqrt{3})\right)$.

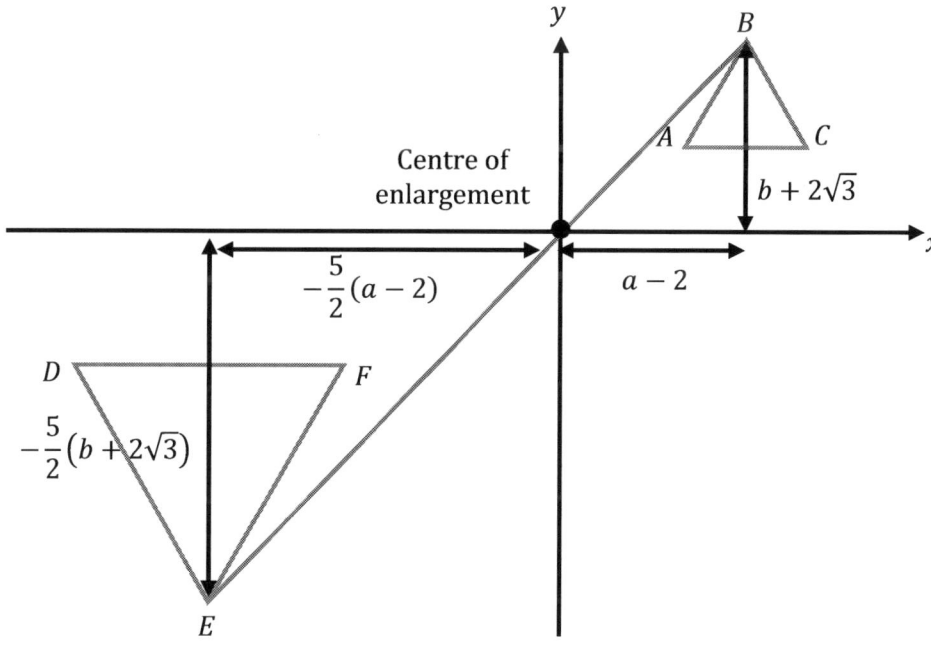

8

We must demonstrate the required result using algebra, so we cannot just substitute different values of n into each sequence and infer a pattern.

We must form an inequality and find the range of values of n for which terms in sequence A are greater than terms in sequence B.

The inequality formed will be a quadratic as shown:

sequence $A >$ sequence B

$2n^2 - 4n + 3 > n^2 - 2n + 3$

$n^2 - 4n + 3 > -2n + 3$ Subtract n^2.

$n^2 - 2n + 3 > 3$ Add $2n$.

$n^2 - 2n > 0$ Subtract 3.

$n(n - 2) > 0$ Factorise.

We now find the critical values (which means we solve the inequality) for the quadratic inequality:
$n(n - 2) = 0$

Either $n = 0$ or $n = 2$.
These are the horizontal axis intercepts of a graph with n on the horizontal axis.
We can demonstrate and interpret a quadratic inequality by plotting a graph.
The equation of the graph will be $y = n(n - 2)$.
We are looking for the regions where $n(n - 2)$ is above the horizontal axis.
The graph of $y = n(n - 2)$ will be a positive quadratic and intercepts the n-axis at 0 and 2.
The regions where $n(n - 2) > 0$ are when $n < 0$ and $n > 2$.

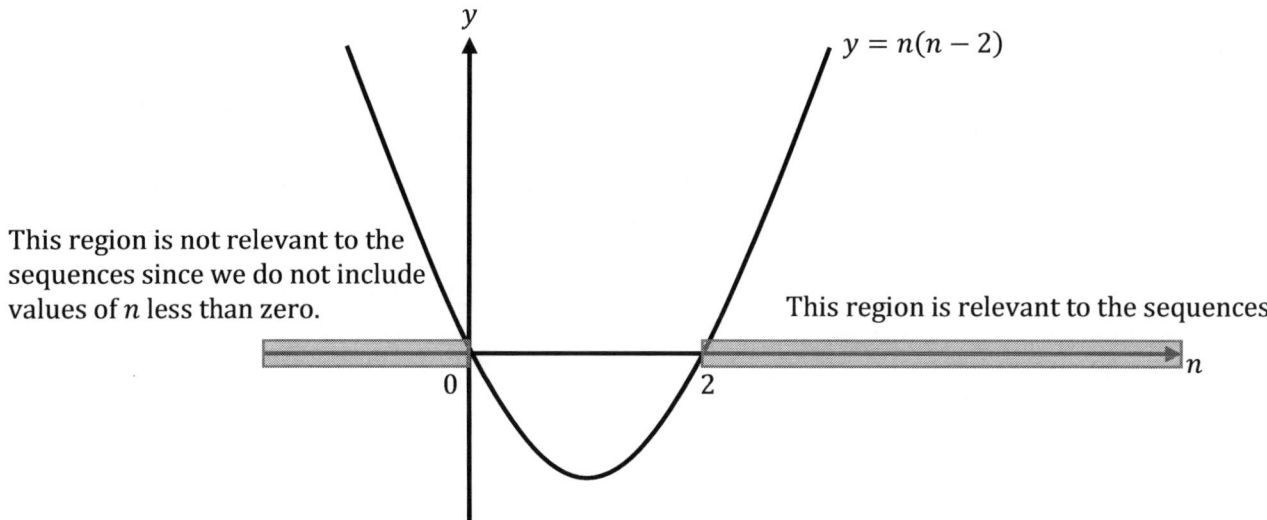

This region is not relevant to the sequences since we do not include values of n less than zero.

This region is relevant to the sequences

The graph clearly shows that sequence $A >$ sequence B when $n > 2$.
Here is a table with the first 5 terms from each sequence.

Sequence	n				
	1	2	3	4	5
$A : 2n^2 - 4n + 3$	1	3	9	19	33
$B : n^2 - 2n + 3$	2	3	6	11	18

We can see that sequence A is greater than sequence B for $n > 2$ which we have proved using inequalities.

9

Below is a general definition of the term "factor":
If x is a factor of y then x must divide y an integer number of times.
From this we can say that if $\left(a^b - 1\right)$ is a factor of $\left(a^{4b} - 1\right)$ then $\left(a^b - 1\right)$ must divide $\left(a^{4b} - 1\right)$ an integer number of times.
Since both are algebraic expressions the only way to find factors is to factorise $\left(a^{4b} - 1\right)$.

We notice that this expression is of the form "difference of two squares", so we can write:
$$\left(a^{4b} - 1\right) = \left(a^{2b} + 1\right)\left(a^{2b} - 1\right)$$

However, the term $\left(a^{2b} - 1\right)$ is also the difference of two squares, so we can factorise further:
$$\left(a^{2b} + 1\right)\left(a^{2b} - 1\right) = \left(a^{2b} + 1\right)\left(a^{b} + 1\right)\left(a^{b} - 1\right)$$

We can now see that the expression contains the factor $\left(a^{b} - 1\right)$.
Therefore $\left(a^{b} - 1\right)$ is a factor of $\left(a^{4b} - 1\right)$.

In terms of algebra we can write:
$$\frac{\left(a^{2b} + 1\right)\left(a^{b} + 1\right)\left(a^{b} - 1\right)}{a^{b} - 1} = \left(a^{2b} + 1\right)\left(a^{b} + 1\right)$$

Since a and b are integers greater than 1, we know that $\left(a^{2b} + 1\right)\left(a^{b} + 1\right)$ will be an integer.

10
This question is based on variation.
There are three variables: chickens, food and hours.
We are told that 1 chicken consumes 1 kilogram of food in 24 hours.
This gives a start point to any proportional calculations we make.
You must always check how the variables are proportionally related.
Chickens and food are directly proportional: more chickens would require more food.
Chickens and time are inversely proportional: more chickens would consume the food in a shorter time.
Food and time are directly proportional: more food means it would take more time to consume.

There are two groups described in the question.
Both consume 21kg food.
The second group consumes the food 2 hours quicker than the first group.
A table showing the proportional changes will be helpful.
For the first group:

Chickens	Food	Hours	
1	1	24	Input the start values.
x	x	24	Chickens and food both multiplied by x.
x	$\dfrac{x}{4}$	6	Food and hours both divided by 4.

Note that the first group has consumed $\frac{x}{4}$ kg of the 21kg available.
This means there will be $\left(21 - \frac{x}{4}\right)$ kg left.
Now we switch to $x - 4$ chickens.

Chickens	Food	Hours	
1	1	24	Input the start values.
$x - 4$	$x - 4$	24	Chickens and food both multiplied by $x - 4$.
$x - 4$	$21 - \dfrac{x}{4}$	$\dfrac{6(84 - x)}{x - 4}$	*Food and hours both multiplied by $\frac{84-x}{4(x-4)}$.

*Remember with proportion that to find a multiplier you divide where you are going by where you came from.

The food had changed from $x - 4$ to $21 - \frac{x}{4}$ so the multiplier is found by:

$$\text{multiplier} = \frac{\text{where you are going}}{\text{where you came from}}$$

$$= \frac{21 - \frac{x}{4}}{x - 4}$$

$$= \frac{\frac{84 - x}{4}}{x - 4}$$

$$= \frac{84 - x}{4(x - 4)}$$

$\frac{21}{1} - \frac{x}{4} = \frac{84 - x}{4}$

If you divide a fraction by another expression, in this case $\frac{84-x}{4} \div (x - 4)$, you can combine the dividing terms into one product in the denominator.

This multiplier is then applied to 24 so we get:

$$24 \times \frac{84 - x}{4(x - 4)} = \frac{6(84 - x)}{x - 4}$$

The 4 in the denominator reduces the 24 multiplier to 6.

We now sum the time taken by the first group to consume the 21kg:

$$\text{time taken by first group} = 6 + \frac{6(84 - x)}{x - 4} \text{ hours}$$

For the second group:

Chickens	Food	Hours	
1	1	24	Input the start values.
$x - 4$	$x - 4$	24	Chickens and food both multiplied by $x - 4$.
$x - 4$	$\frac{x - 4}{4}$	6	Food and hours both divided by 4.

Note that the second group has consumed $\frac{x-4}{4}$ kg of the 21kg available.

This means there will be $\left(21 - \frac{x-4}{4}\right)$ kg left.

Now we switch to x chickens.

Chickens	Food	Hours	
1	1	24	Input the start values.
x	x	24	Chickens and food both multiplied by x.
x	$21 - \frac{x - 4}{4}$	$\frac{6(88 - x)}{x}$	**Food and hours both multiplied by $\frac{88-x}{4x}$.

**Remember with proportion that to find a multiplier you divide where you are going by where you came from.

The food had changed from x to $21 - \frac{x-4}{4}$ so the multiplier is found by:

$$\text{multiplier} = \frac{\text{where you are going}}{\text{where you came from}}$$

$$= \frac{21 - \frac{x - 4}{4}}{x}$$

$$= \frac{\frac{84 - (x - 4)}{4}}{x}$$

$\frac{21}{1} - \frac{x - 4}{4} = \frac{84 - (x - 4)}{4}$

Watch out for the double negative when you expand the brackets.

If you divide a fraction by another expression, in this case $\frac{84-(x-4)}{4} \div x$, you can combine the dividing terms into one product in the denominator.

$$= \frac{84 - x + 4}{4x}$$

$$= \frac{88 - x}{4x}$$

This multiplier is then applied to 24 so we get:

$$24 \times \frac{88 - x}{4x} = \frac{6(88 - x)}{x}$$

The 4 in the denominator reduces the 24 multiplier to 6.

We now sum the time taken by the second group to consume the 21kg:

$$\text{time taken by second group} = 6 + \frac{6(88 - x)}{x} \text{ hours}$$

Now we can link the times taken by each group together and then solve for x.

time taken by first group = time taken by second group + 2

$$6 + \frac{6(84 - x)}{x - 4} = 6 + \frac{6(88 - x)}{x} + 2$$

$$\frac{6(84 - x)}{x - 4} = \frac{6(88 - x)}{x} + 2$$

Cancel the 6 from both sides.

$$\frac{6(84 - x)}{x - 4} = \frac{6(88 - x) + 2x}{x}$$

$$\frac{6(88 - x)}{x} + \frac{2}{1} = \frac{6(88 - x) + 2x}{x}$$

Expand the brackets in the right hand side numerator.

$$\frac{6(84 - x)}{x - 4} = \frac{528 - 6x + 2x}{x}$$

$$\frac{6(84 - x)}{x - 4} = \frac{528 - 4x}{x}$$

Collect the terms.

$$6x(84 - x) = (528 - 4x)(x - 4)$$

Multiply by $(x - 4)$ and x to remove the denominators.

$$504x - 6x^2 = 528x - 2112 - 4x^2 + 16x$$

Expand the brackets.

$$0 = 2x^2 + 40x - 2112$$

Add $6x^2$, subtract $504x$ and simplify the terms. Set the quadratic equal to zero.

$$x^2 + 20x - 1056 = 0$$

Divide by 2.

$$(x - 24)(x + 44) = 0$$

Factorise or use the quadratic formula. Reject the negative solution $x = -44$.

Since x is a positive number the correct solution is $x = 24$.

Exercise 9

1

A and B are fixed points.
Point C is free to move around the points A and B.
If $AC^2 + BC^2 = AB^2$, construct the locus of points of C.

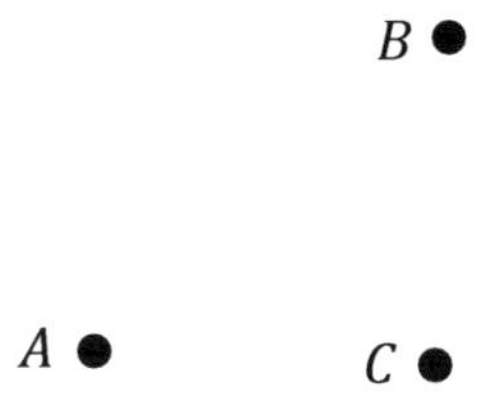

B ●

A ● C ●

2

A man and a cyclist travel in a straight line towards each other.
The man starts at A and the cyclist from B, both starting at 2pm and they both continue until they meet.
On another day the cyclist sets off at 2pm but the man starts walking some time later.
Both the man and the cyclist meet 3 minutes later than normal.
The man walks at 6km/h and the cyclist cycles at 30km/h.
The distance AB is 36km.
What time did the man set off walking?

Man A ————————————————————— B Cyclist

3

The diagram shows a semicircle with centre O and radius OM shown by b.
N is the midpoint of OM.
A smaller circle of radius a is drawn inside the semicircle.
The radius of the semicircle forms a tangent to the small circle at N.
The semicircle touches the small circle at the point P.
Find the ratio $a : b$ in its simplest form.

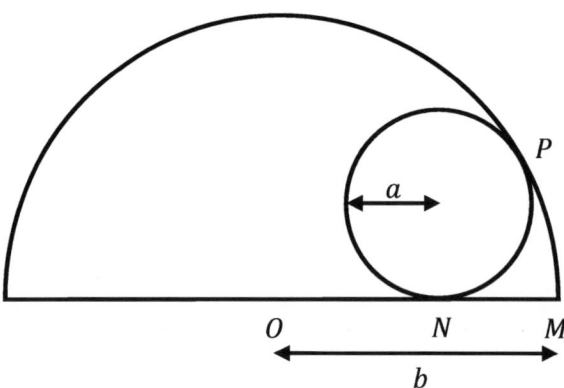

4 calculator

The diagram shows the journey made by a ship as it responded to a distress call.
XPY is a horizontal line of length 48km.
AX is 15km, BY is 21km and both are perpendicular to the line XPY.
AX and BY are parallel to North.
The ship travels from point A on a bearing of $(180 - \alpha)°$ to reach point P.
$\alpha < 90°$
The ship then turns anticlockwise by $(180 - 2\alpha)°$ and continues from P towards B.
Find the distance XP.

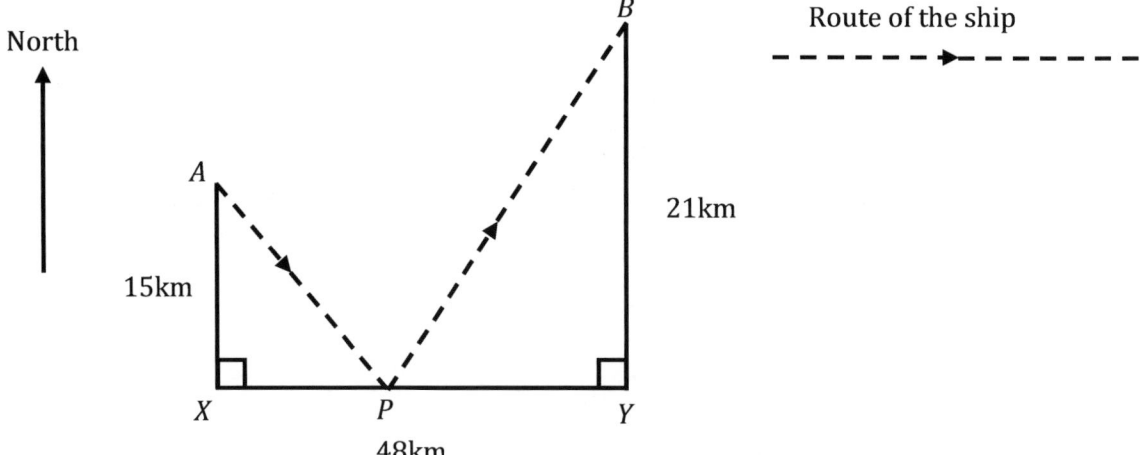

5

The product of three consecutive even numbers is added to x times the middle even number.
This is identical to the cube of the middle even number.
Find the value of x.

6

60 pupils took an exam in mathematics and an exam in physics.
The table below shows the results

	Pass	Fail
Mathematics	50	10
Physics	44	16

It is given that 4 pupils failed both exams.
Find the number of pupils who passed both exams.

7

Curve A has the equation $y = 5^{2x}$.
Curve B is formed from two transformations applied to curve A.
Find the equation of curve B.

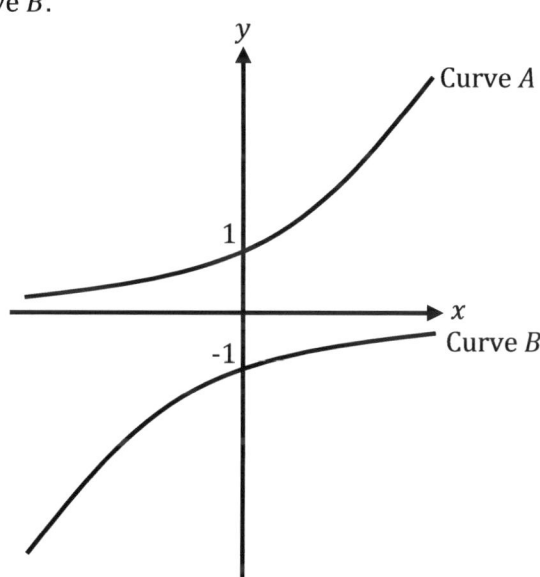

8 calculator

A survey of x people is carried out from those who purchased tickets to a flower show.
The show was held in May, June and July.
The flower show costs £9.60 per person but there is a 10% June discount with a voucher.
Of those surveyed,

   40% went in May.

   25% of the people surveyed used a voucher.

The ratio of men to women surveyed in June is 3 : 4
$\frac{1}{4}$ of the males in June used a voucher.

$\frac{3}{4}$ of the females in June used a voucher.

The July tickets totalled £384.
The mean amount spent per ticket was £9.36.
Find the value of x.

9

In the Venn diagram, shade the region defined by $(A \cap B) \cup (A \cap C)$.

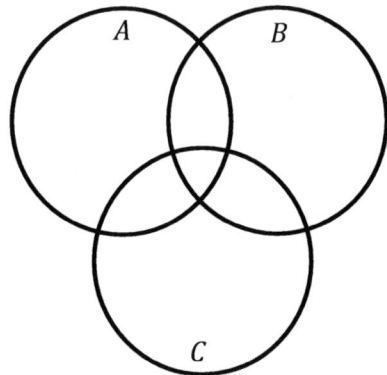

10 calculator

At a science conference a student examined the number of languages spoken by the people attending three different lectures.
The results are shown in the bar chart below.

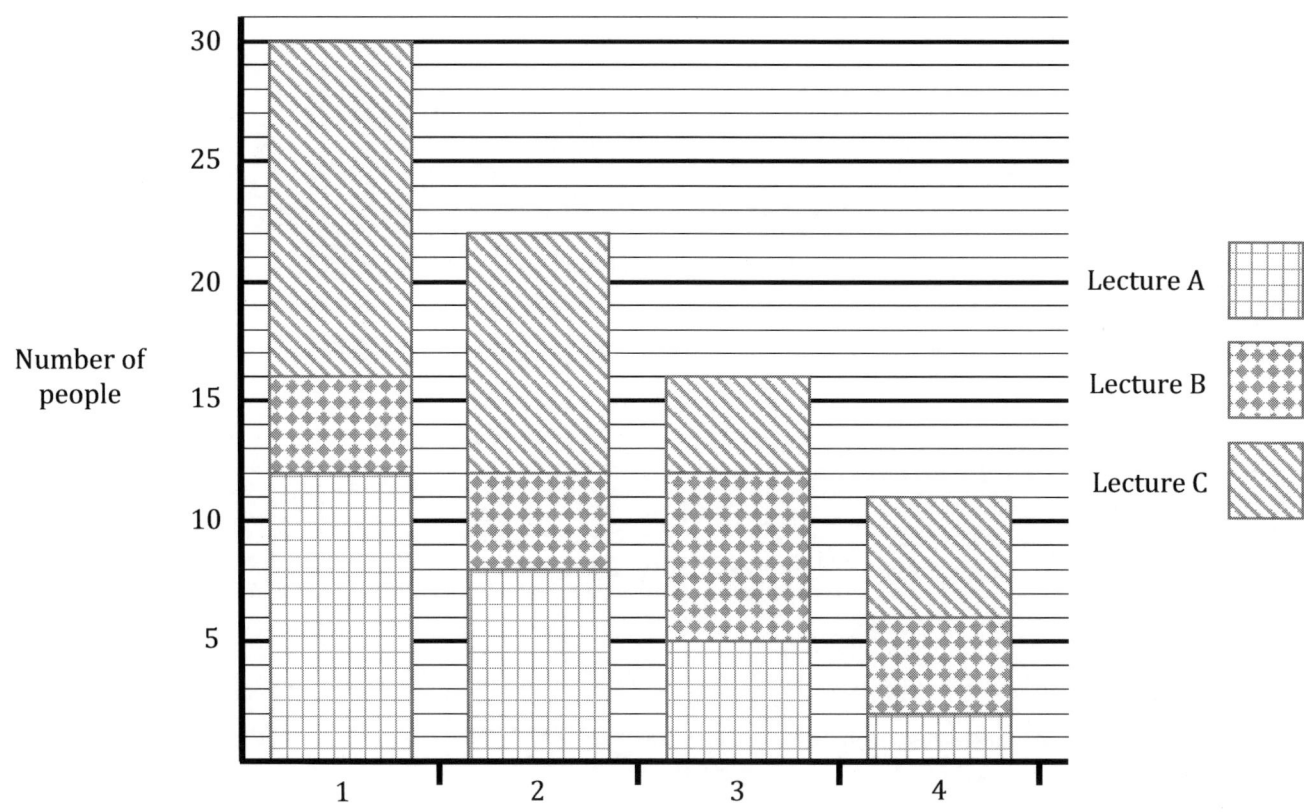

Number of languages spoken

Which of these probabilities is greater:

Of those who spoke more than 1 language a person was in the lecture with the smallest number of people.

Being in a lecture where more than 40% of people speak more than 2 languages.

Exercise 9 Solutions

1

The equation $AC^2 + BC^2 = AB^2$ is describing the Pythagorean theorem.

This implies there will be a right angle at point C.

Point C is free to move but there must always be a right angle at C formed from the lines AC and BC.

The locus of points for C will describe a circle with diameter AB.

The circle theorem states that a triangle formed in a semicircle will be right-angled.

A semicircle will include one side as a diameter.

In this case the diameter will be AB.

We can form the locus of points for C by constructing a circle of diameter AB that goes through all the points A, B and C.

The circumference will be the locus of points for C.

We need to find the centre of AB which will be the centre of the circle.

We find the centre by constructing a perpendicular bisector of line AB.

Draw a line joining AB.

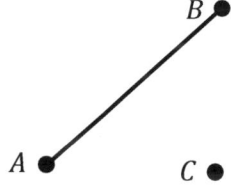

Set the compass length to AB.

Draw an arc from A and an arc from B until the arcs cross.

The points where the arcs cross are X and Y.

Join the line XY so that it crosses AB.

Call the crossing point P.

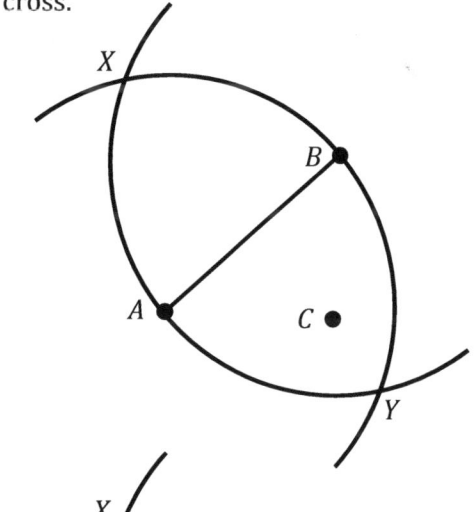

The point of intersection of the lines AB and XY is the centre of the circle.
Set the compass length to AP and place the compass point at P.
Complete the circle passing through A, B and C.
The construction is now complete.

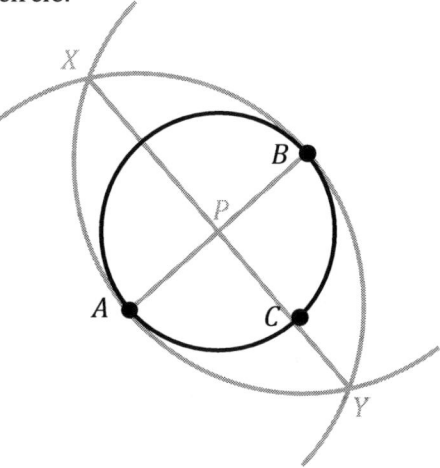

Point C can be moved anywhere on the circumference and it will always form a right angle with AC and BC.

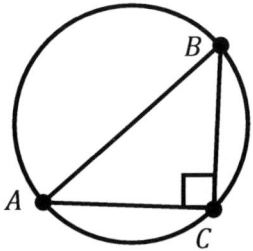 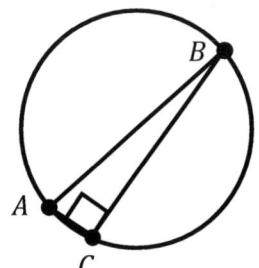 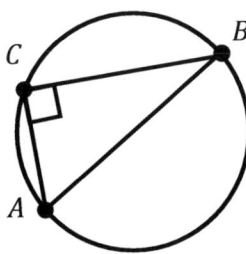

2

We need to model two scenarios for this question:
The first is the normal start time and distances travelled.
The second is the unknown start time for the man and the new distances travelled.
If two objects are moving towards each other with known speeds and known separation, we can determine how long it would take for them to meet.
The man travels at 6km/h and the cyclist at 30km/h.
They would approach each other at a combined speed of $6 + 30 = 36$km/h.
The distance travelled is 36km, so we can calculate the time taken to meet:

$$\text{time} = \frac{\text{distance}}{\text{speed}}$$
$$= \frac{36}{36}$$
$$= 1$$

The man and cyclist normally meet 1 hour after they start travelling (3pm).
We can also calculate how far each normally travels in this time:

$$\text{distance travelled by man} = \text{speed of man} \times \text{time}$$
$$= 6 \times 1$$
$$= 6\text{km}$$

$$\text{distance travelled by cyclist} = \text{speed of cyclist} \times \text{time}$$
$$= 30 \times 1$$
$$= 30\text{km}$$

In the second scenario the cyclist still sets off at 2pm but must travel for an extra 3 minutes before meeting the man.

This means we can calculate the distance that the cyclist travelled.

Also note that 3 minutes must be divided by 60 to be consistent with hours.

This means the cyclist would travel for $1\frac{3}{60}$ hours before meeting the man.

The speed of the cyclist has not changed.

distance cyclist travels in second scenario = speed × time

$$= 30 \times 1\frac{3}{60}$$
$$= 31.5$$

The cyclist travels 31.5km.

The difference between 36km and 31.5km will be the distance the man walked: $36 - 31.5 = 4.5$km.

Note that the time of meeting in the second scenario is 3:03pm.

Any time we calculate for the man will need to be subtracted from this time.

The speed of the man has not changed.

$$\text{time man walked} = \frac{\text{distance man walked}}{\text{speed of man}}$$
$$= \frac{4.5}{6}$$
$$= 0.75\text{hrs}$$

This would be a travel time of 45 minutes.

So the man set off 45 minutes before 3:03pm, which would have been 2:18pm.

The man started walking at 2:18pm.

The diagram below can help visualise the question.

First scenario

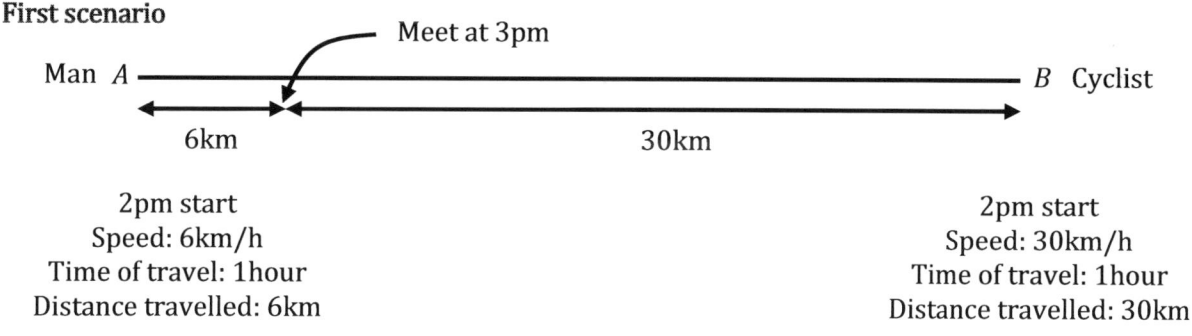

Second scenario

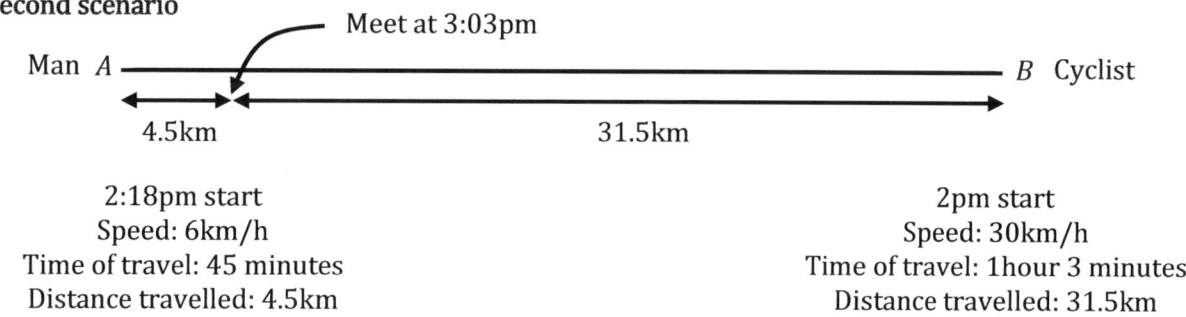

3

We need to find an equation to link a and b before we can find the ratio $a : b$

Radii can be measured from the centre of a circle in any direction.

We know that $OP = b$ since it is also a radius of the semicircle.

The line OP cuts the small circle at two points.

One of them is point P but the other we can call Q.

The line OP is formed from $2a$ and the distance OQ.

Let $OQ = x$

We know that OM is a tangent to the small circle touching at the point N.

This means that the centre of the small circle to the point N (which has distance a) will be perpendicular to the tangent OM.

The distance $ON = \frac{1}{2}b$ as given in the question.

We now have a link using a right-angled triangle and Pythagoras.

$$(a + x)^2 = a^2 + \left(\frac{1}{2}b\right)^2$$ 　Use the Pythagorean relation $A^2 + B^2 = C^2$.

$$(a + x)(a + x) = a^2 + \frac{1}{4}b^2$$ 　Expand the brackets.

$$a^2 + ax + ax + x^2 = a^2 + \frac{1}{4}b^2$$ 　Cancel the a^2 terms from both sides.

$$2ax + x^2 = \frac{1}{4}b^2 \quad [1]$$ 　Collect the terms.

We need to eliminate x to find the ratio for a and b.

This means we need another equation.

We know that $OP = OM$, so we can say $b = 2a + x$.

Making x the subject, we can say $x = b - 2a$ [2]

Now we substitute equation [2] into [1]:

$$2a(b - 2a) + (b - 2a)^2 = \frac{1}{4}b^2$$ 　Replace x with $b - 2a$.

$$2ab - 4a^2 + (b - 2a)(b - 2a) = \frac{1}{4}b^2$$ 　Expand the brackets.

$$2ab - 4a^2 + b^2 - 2ab - 2ab + 4a^2 = \frac{1}{4}b^2$$

$$b^2 - 2ab = \frac{1}{4}b^2$$ 　Collect the terms; notice $4a^2$ cancels out.

$$b - 2a = \frac{1}{4}b$$ 　Divide by b (we know b is not zero).

$$2a = \frac{3}{4}b$$ 　Subtract $\frac{1}{4}b$ and add $2a$.

$$8a = 3b$$ 　Multiply by 4.

Using ratio cross multiplication the ratio $a : b = 3 : 8$

Cross multiplying a ratio

$$8a = 3b$$

$a : b$

$3 : 8$

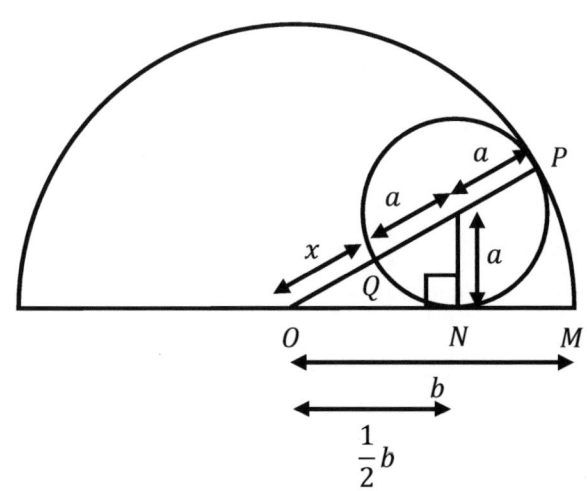

4

We need to find the distance XP.

We know two things about the triangle AXP, the 90° angle and the side $AX = 15$km.

In general, you need to know a mixture of three angles and sides in a triangle before you can calculate any other sides and angles.

We are given some bearings in terms of α.

We start by adding these to the diagram.

The first bearing $(180 - \alpha)°$ of P from A shows the initial direction of the ship.

This means that angle XAP can be found because it is on a straight line parallel to North.

$$\text{angle } XAP = 180 - (180 - \alpha)$$
$$= 180 - 180 + \alpha$$
$$= \alpha$$

If we then draw a perpendicular line from P in the direction of North we can form the angle between AP and North.

This will also be α because it is alternate to angle XAP.

The ship then turns anticlockwise by $(180 - 2\alpha)°$ to face in the direction PB.

We can calculate the angle APB:

$$\text{angle } APB = 180 - (180 - 2\alpha)$$
$$= 180 - 180 + 2\alpha$$
$$= 2\alpha$$

We already know the angle between AP and North is α.

Since angle $APB = 2\alpha$ we can say the angle between PB and North must be α.

By alternate angles we also know angle $PBY = \alpha$.

Since two angles are confirmed as equal in both triangles AXP and BPY, the third angle must also be the same; let that angle be β.

Triangles AXP and BPY are similar triangles, which means the ratio of their sides are equal and we can form and solve an equation.

Let $XP = x$, then $PY = 48 - x$ since XY is 48km.

Route of the ship

North

$180 - \alpha$

A

α

B

α

21km

15km

α α

β β

X x P $180 - 2\alpha$ $48 - x$ Y

48km

When forming equations from similar triangles we must identify the corresponding sides.

These are found by checking which two angles are formed at the end of the side.

AX corresponds to BY as they are between the angles 90° and α.

XP corresponds to PY as they are between the angles 90° and β.

We can say:

$$\frac{x}{15} = \frac{48 - x}{21}$$

$21x = 15(48 - x)$	Multiply by 15 and 21.
$7x = 5(48 - x)$	Divide by 3.
$7x = 240 - 5x$	Expand the brackets.
$12x = 240$	Add $5x$.
$x = 20$	Divide by 12.

The correct answer is 20km.

5

We need to convert the question into algebra:

product of 3 consecutive even numbers $+ x \times$ middle number $= $ (middle number)^3

The general even number can be represented by $2n$.

Even numbers differ by 2.

When considering three consecutive even numbers in terms of algebra we can write: $2n - 2, 2n$ and $2n + 2$

This sometimes works out more efficient than writing $2n, 2n + 2$ and $2n + 4$.

The product of the three consecutive even numbers will be $(2n - 2) \times 2n \times (2n + 2)$.

This product is added to x times the middle even number: $x \times 2n$.

So far we have: $(2n - 2) \times 2n \times (2n + 2) + x \times 2n$.

We are told that this is identical to the cube of the middle number: $(2n)^3$.

Now we can form the identity:

$(2n - 2) \times 2n \times (2n + 2) + x \times 2n \equiv (2n)^3$

The identity means that the left hand side is a rearrangement of the right hand side.

It is not the same as an equation so we approach identities in a different way.

We start with the left hand side and begin simplifying the terms:

$$\begin{aligned}
\text{left hand side} &= (2n - 2) \times 2n \times (2n + 2) + x \times 2n \\
&= 2n(2n + 2)(2n - 2) + 2xn \\
&= 2n(4n^2 - 4) + 2xn \\
&= 8n^3 - 8n + 2xn
\end{aligned}$$

Note that $(2n + 2)(2n - 2) = 4n^2 - 4$ is the difference of two squares.

Expand the brackets.

The right hand side of the identity simplifies to $8n^3$.

If the simplified left hand side is identical to the right hand side then the numbers in front of the powers of n must be the same.

This is a process called equating coefficients.

The coefficient of n^3 on the left hand side is 8.

We can see that this is identical to the coefficient of n^3 on the right hand side.

The coefficient of n on the left hand side is $-8 + 2x$.

The coefficient of n on the right hand side is 0; there is no n term.

The coefficients must be equal in an identity so we can write:

$$\begin{aligned}
-8 + 2x &= 0 \\
2x &= 8 \\
x &= 4
\end{aligned}$$

The correct value of x is 4.

6

The data is presented in a two-way table.

It can also be presented in a Venn diagram.

Let $\xi = 60$ pupils who took the exams

M is the pupils who passed the maths exam

P is the pupils who passed the physics exam.

Let the number who passed the maths exam only be a.

Let the number who passed both exams be b.

Let the number who passed the physics exam only be c.

We know that 4 students failed both exams.

We can say that $a + b + c = 56$ [1].

We know that $a + b = 50$ [2].

We know that $b + c = 44$ [3]

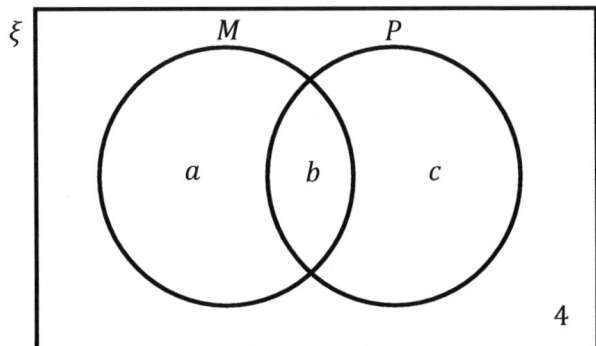

We can substitute equation [2] into [1]:

$(a + b) + c = 56$

$\quad 50 + c = 56$

$\qquad\quad c = 6$

Now we can substitute $c = 6$ into equation [3]:

$b + c = 44$

$b + 6 = 44$

$\quad\ b = 38$

38 students passed both maths and physics.

7

The curve has been rotated 180 degrees about the origin.

This can be achieved by successively reflecting the curve in both the y and x-axis.

Let the curve A equation be defined by $f(x) = 5^{2x}$

A reflection in the y-axis is represented by $f(-x)$, this would change the equation to:

$f(-x) = 5^{2(-x)}$

$\qquad\quad = 5^{-2x}$

A reflection in the x-axis is represented by $-f(x)$.

Since we have already reflected in the y-axis we would have $-f(-x)$, this would change the equation to:

$-f(-x) = -5^{-2x}$

This is the equation of curve B: $y = -5^{-2x}$.

Reflect in the y-axis

$$f(x) \rightarrow f(-x)$$

Reflect in the x-axis

$$f(-x) \rightarrow -f(-x)$$

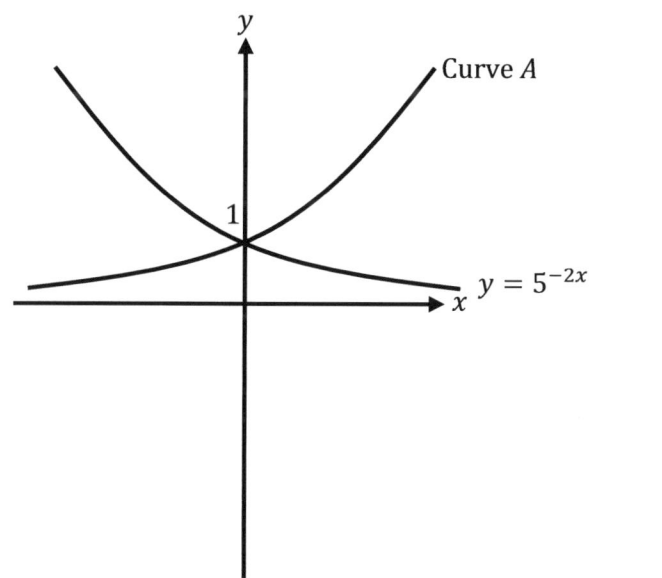

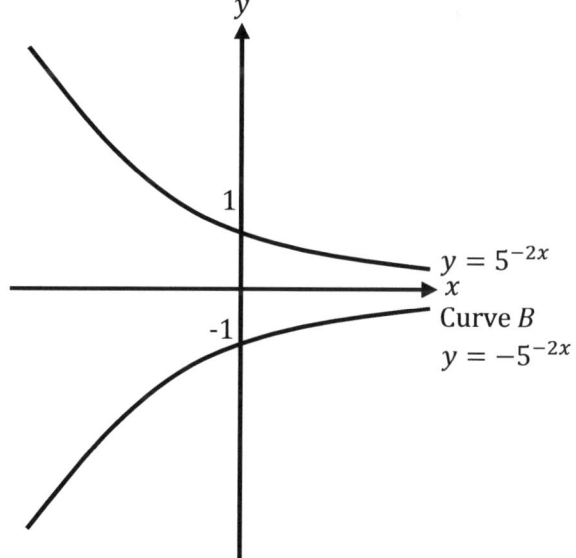

8

We have three months that the flower show was attended and this is split into male/female.

We can express the information in a two-way table.

This will make the given information easier to interpret.

There are x people altogether.

40% went in May which will be $0.4x$ since 0.4 is the multiplier for 40%.
Call the number of males in June $3a$ and the number of females in June $4a$.
This is because the ratio given for male : female $= 3 : 4$ in June.
a is the multiplier that produces the actual numbers of male and females in June.
We have two variables, a and x, that we need to determine.
This implies that we need two equations that connect them.
One equation can link the total costs for the people surveyed.
The other can link the number of people who had a voucher.
The two-way table is shown below with extra information from further calculations:

	Male	Female	Number of people	Amount spent (£)
May			$0.4x$	$0.4x \times 9.6 = 3.84x$
June	$3a$	$4a$	$7a$	$6.48a + 25.92a + 31.2a = 63.6a$
July				384
Total			x	$9.36x$

We know the mean amount spent per person was £9.36.
Since there were x people in total the product $9.36x$ will represent the total amount spent.
We can break this cost down into people who paid the normal price, £9.60, and those who paid with a 10% discount; this would be £8.64 (9.60×0.9).
The amount spent in May will be $0.4x \times 9.6 = 3.84x$ since they all paid the normal price.
The amount spent in July was given as £384.
The amount spent in June will be split into those who used a voucher and those who did not.
$\frac{1}{4}$ of the males in June used a voucher.
Since the number of males in June is $3a$, the number who used a voucher will be $3a \times \frac{1}{4} = \frac{3}{4}a$.
The amount spent by the males in June with a voucher will be $\frac{3}{4}a \times 8.64 = 6.48a$.
$\frac{3}{4}$ of the females in June used a voucher.
Since the number of females in June is $4a$, the number who used a voucher will be $4a \times \frac{3}{4} = 3a$.
The amount spent by the females in June with a voucher will be $3a \times 8.64 = 25.92a$.
Now we total the amount spent by those in June who did not have a voucher.
There were $7a$ people in June, of which $\frac{3}{4}a + 3a = \frac{15}{4}a$ people had vouchers.
The remainder will be those who paid the normal price of £9.60.
The remaining people in June will be $7a - \frac{15}{4}a = \frac{13}{4}a$.
The remaining people in June spent $\frac{13}{4}a \times 9.60 = 31.2a$

Now we can form an equation with a and x for the total costs:
$$\text{May spend} + \text{June spend} + \text{July spend} = 9.36x$$
$$\text{May spend} + \text{male with voucher June} + \text{female with voucher June} + \text{people without voucher June} + \text{July spend} = 9.36x$$
$$3.84x + 6.48a + 25.92a + 31.2a + 384 = 9.36x$$
$$3.84x + 63.6a + 384 = 9.36x$$
$$63.6a + 384 = 5.52x \quad [1]$$

For the second equation, we can link the percentage of people who used a voucher with a and x.
We know that $\frac{15}{4}a$ people used a voucher and we know this is 25% of the total number of people, $\frac{1}{4}x$.
We can equate these values for the second equation:
$$\frac{15}{4}a = \frac{1}{4}x$$
$$15a = x$$

$$a = \frac{1}{15}x \quad [2]$$

We can substitute equation [2] into [1]:

$$63.6a + 384 = 5.52x$$
$$63.6\left(\frac{1}{15}x\right) + 384 = 5.52x$$
$$4.24x + 384 = 5.52x$$
$$1.28x = 384$$
$$x = 300$$

There were 300 people in the survey.

9

The symbol ∩ means the intersection of two sets.

It can be thought of as requiring that the area is in both sets at the same time.

So $A \cap B$ means the area that is both A and B (not either/or).

The symbol ∪ means the union of two sets.

It can be thought of as requiring that the area is in either of the sets, or both at the same time.

So $A \cup B$ means the area that is A or B or both.

We are given $(A \cap B) \cup (A \cap C)$ which we can think of as the union of $A \cap B$ and $A \cap C$.

$A \cap B$ defines this region

$A \cap C$ defines this region

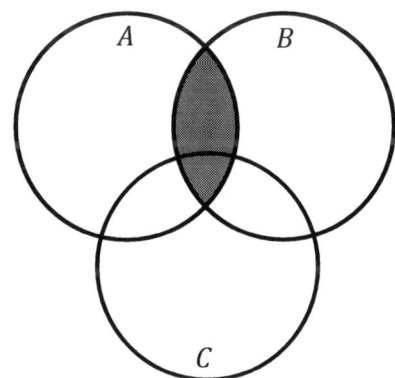

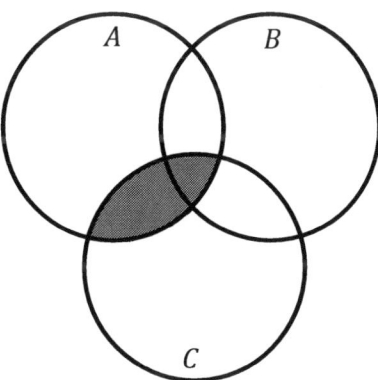

Each of $A \cap B$ and $A \cap C$ can be thought of as their own sets.

Since we are asked to show the region $(A \cap B) \cup (A \cap C)$, we just combine the two together to give the correct answer shown below:

$(A \cap B) \cup (A \cap C)$ defines this region

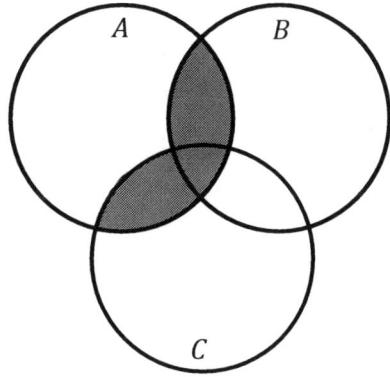

10

Composite bar charts can be shown in a two-way table.
The columns will be the lectures and the rows will be the number of languages spoken.

	Lecture A	Lecture B	Lecture C	Totals
1 language	12	4	14	30
2 languages	8	4	10	22
3 languages	5	7	4	16
4 languages	2	4	5	11
Totals	27	19	33	79

Now we can interpret the probabilities:
The first probability:
"Of those who spoke more than 1 language a person was in the lecture with the smallest number of people".
The number of people who spoke more than one language will be $22 + 16 + 11 = 49$.
The number of people who spoke more than one language and were in the lecture with the smallest number of people will be $4 + 7 + 4 = 15$.
The required probability is $\frac{15}{49}$.

The second probability:
"Being in a lecture where more than 40% of people speak more than 2 languages".

The number of people in lecture A who speak more than 2 languages will be $5 + 2 = 7$.
As a percentage of people in lecture A we obtain: $\frac{7}{27} \times 100 = 25.9\%$
Lecture A has below the 40% requirement.

The number of people in lecture B who speak more than 2 languages will be $7 + 4 = 11$.
As a percentage of people in lecture B we obtain: $\frac{11}{19} \times 100 = 57.9\%$
Lecture B has above the 40% requirement.

The number of people in lecture C who speak more than 2 languages will be $4 + 5 = 9$.
As a percentage of people in lecture C we obtain: $\frac{9}{33} \times 100 = 27.3\%$
Lecture C has below the 40% requirement.

Since this probability is taken from the entire population of 79 we get a probability of $\frac{19}{79}$ for being in a lecture where more than 40% of people speak more than 2 languages.

Comparing values we can see that $\frac{15}{49} > \frac{19}{79}$ (0.306 > 0.241).

The correct answer is:
"Of those who spoke more than 1 language a person was in the lecture with the smallest number of people".

Exercise 10

1

Some letters are shown on the cards below.
The letters can be arranged to form six-letter combinations.
It is required that the six-letter combination must have two vowels at the start and one vowel at the end.
How many six-letter combinations can be created?

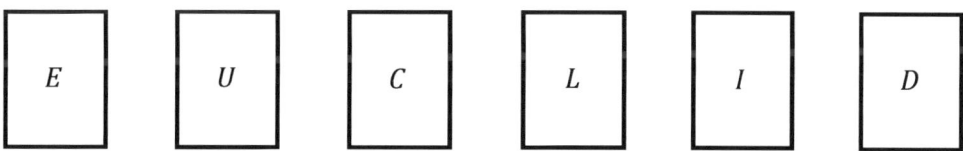

2 calculator

How many ways can 1155 be written as the product of two factors?

3 calculator

A quiz contains 10 questions that can be answered true or false.
If all questions are attempted, how many different ways can the questions be answered?

4 calculator

A delivery driver has to make deliveries on 3 days.
The table shows the number of different delivery destinations required on each day.

Day	Number of deliveries
1	4
2	5
3	6

The delivery which is furthest from the depot is always done first on each day.
The driver can then chose the order in which to complete the other deliveries of the day.
How many different ways can the driver deliver to all the destinations on all 3 days?

5

A set of variables are related by the equation:

$$\frac{3h + b}{5h + c} = \frac{x}{y}$$

If b and c are increased by the same amount, the value of h is unaffected.
Find the ratio $x : y$

6 calculator

Three factories build the same type of aircraft.
 Factory A completes an aircraft every 8 weeks.
 Factory B completes an aircraft every 12 weeks.
 Factory C completes an aircraft every 6 weeks.

The factories can work together to complete an aircraft.
How much quicker, in days, would A and C working together be than A and B working together to complete an aircraft?

7 calculator

A water tank is connected to three pipes.
Two of the pipes fill the tank and the other empties the tank.
The following values show the times if one pipe is operating on its own:
 Pipe X fills the tank completely in 16 hours.
 Pipe Y fills the tank completely in 30 hours.
 Pipe Z empties the tank completely in x hours.

If all three pipes are operating at the same time it will take 80 hours to fill the tank.
Find the value of x.

8

Three positive integers, a, b and c, are chosen.
b is three times a and c is two times b.
The mean of the reciprocals of the integers is $\frac{1}{8}$.
Find a, b and c.

9

When the integer x is divided by 6 the remainder is 5.
What will the remainder be when x^2 is divided by 6?

10 calculator

A rectangular bathroom of area 86400cm^2 is being tiled.
n small rectangular tiles of length to width ratio $4 : 3$ are required to tile the bathroom.
It requires 20 less tiles to tile the bathroom when a large rectangular tile of length to width ratio $6 : 5$ is used.
The large tile has an area 48cm^2 greater than the small tile.
The tiles do not overlap.
Find the value of n.

Exercise 10 Solutions

1

We are told that there must be two vowels at the start and one at the end.

The position of the vowels in the six-letter combination does not actually matter.

What is important is that there are 3 vowels, E, U and I, that can be arranged in any order that happen to be in fixed positions overall (1st, 2nd and last positions).

The number of ways of arranging 3 different objects is 6.

This comes from the calculation $3 \times 2 \times 1 = 6$.

In general, the number of ways of arranging n different objects is given by $n(n-1)(n-2) \ldots \times 2 \times 1$.

So you multiply by every integer from n down to 1.

The other 3 letters (C, L and D) can also be arranged in any order about fixed positions (3rd, 4th and 5th).

So we can say the number of ways of arranging these 3 letters is 6 for the same reason as above.

Overall we have two groups of 3 letters that can each be arranged in 6 different ways.

The total number of six-letter combinations will be $6 \times 6 = 36$.

The correct answer is 36.

Here are all the combinations:

EICDLU	EICLDU	EIDCLU	EIDLCU	EILCDU	EILDCU
EUCDLI	EUCLDI	EUDCLI	EUDLCI	EULCDI	EULDCI
IECDLU	IECLDU	IEDCLU	IEDLCU	IELCDU	IELDCU
IUCDLE	IUCLDE	IUDCLE	IUDLCE	IULCDE	IULDCE
UECDLI	UECLDI	UEDCLI	UEDLCI	UELCDI	UELDCI
UICDLE	UICLDE	UIDCLE	UIDLCE	UILCDE	UILDCE

2

There are two ways to find the factors of a number.

The first is just to try and list all the factors in order from 1×1155 onwards.

This method can take a while to complete.

The second is to write 1155 as a product of its prime factors and then pair them together such that you have two factors (and then also include 1×1155 since 1 is not a prime).

1155 has a factor of 5 since it ends in 5:
$$1155 = 5 \times 231$$

231 has a factor of 3 since its digits sum to 6 ($2 + 3 + 1 = 6$), which is a multiple of 3:
$$1155 = 5 \times 3 \times 77$$

77 has factors 7 and 11 which are both prime:
$$1155 = 5 \times 3 \times 7 \times 11$$
$$= 3 \times 5 \times 7 \times 11$$

Now we need to combine these factors together to form two factors.

There are 4 prime numbers here so we can start by forming 1 prime multiplied by a product of 3 primes, and 2 primes multiplied by a product of 2 primes as follows:

$$\left.\begin{array}{l} 3 \times (5 \times 7 \times 11) \\ 5 \times (3 \times 7 \times 11) \\ 7 \times (3 \times 5 \times 11) \\ 11 \times (3 \times 5 \times 7) \end{array}\right\} \quad \text{4 products}$$

Remember that each product of three primes will be the same number regardless of order; $5 \times 7 \times 11$ will be the same as $11 \times 7 \times 5$.

Now we can find the product of 2 primes multiplied by a product of 2 primes:

$$(3 \times 5) \times (7 \times 11)$$
$$(3 \times 7) \times (5 \times 11) \left.\right\} \text{ 3 products}$$
$$(3 \times 11) \times (5 \times 7)$$

Don't forget 1×1155.

The total number of ways is $4 + 3 + 1 = 8$
The correct answer is 8.
Here are all the factors of 1155:
$1, 3, 5, 7, 11, 15, 21, 33, 35, 55, 77, 105, 165, 231, 385,$ and 1155

3
Each question has 2 outcomes: true or false.
This means that for each question answered, the number of possible outcomes increases by a factor of 2.
Since there are 10 questions the number of possible outcomes will be 2^{10}.
The correct answer is 1024.
In this type of problem, the order of the events matters.
By this we mean that true then false is different to false then true.
In certain questions the order of the events does not matter.
Suppose there was a raffle and there were (to keep the numbers manageable) 4 tickets sold to different people, A, B, C and D.
Say two of the people were winners.
If you were asked "how many different pairings of winners could there be", you would need to recognise that AB and BA would be the same and would only count as one pairing.
The number of combinations would be 6: AB, AC, AD, BC, BD and CD.

4
This question combines both the number of ways objects can be ordered and the product rule for counting.
We first consider the number of different orders in which the deliveries could be done on each day.
We note that the furthest delivery is done first.
This has the effect of reducing the number of choices to order on each day by 1.
Day 1 has 4 deliveries, but since the first delivery is fixed we are really looking at ordering the other 3 deliveries.
The number of ways of arranging 3 different objects is 6; this comes from $3 \times 2 \times 1 = 6$.
In general, the number of ways of arranging n objects is given by $n(n - 1)(n - 2) \dots \times 2 \times 1$.
So you multiply by every integer from n down to 1.

Day 2 has 5 deliveries, but since the first delivery is fixed we are looking at the other 4 deliveries.
The number of ways of arranging 4 different objects is 24; this comes from $4 \times 3 \times 2 \times 1 = 24$.
Day 3 has 6 deliveries, but since the first delivery is fixed we are looking at the other 5 deliveries.
The number of ways of arranging 5 different objects is 120; this comes from $5 \times 4 \times 3 \times 2 \times 1 = 120$.

We now consider the product rule for counting.
There are 6 options for day 1, 24 options for day 2 and 120 options for day 3.
All of these can be combined in any way.
To find the number of combinations we multiply each of the numbers together (the product):
$6 \times 24 \times 120 = 17280$

The correct answer is 17280.

5

The question states that b and c can be increased by the same amount without any effect on the value of h.
This statement is describing an equation for us to form.
We need to make h the subject of the original equation:

$$\frac{3h+b}{5h+c} = \frac{x}{y}$$

$$3h+b = \frac{x(5h+c)}{y} \qquad \text{Multiply by } (5h+c).$$

$$y(3h+b) = x(5h+c) \qquad \text{Multiply by } y.$$

$$3hy + by = 5hx + cx \qquad \text{Expand the brackets.}$$

$$3hy - 5hx = cx - by \qquad \text{Collect the } h \text{ terms on the left hand side.}$$

$$h(3y - 5x) = cx - by \qquad \text{Factorise for } h.$$

$$h = \frac{cx - by}{3y - 5x} \quad [1] \qquad \text{Divide by } (3y - 5x).$$

This equation represents the value of h.
We now increase b and c by the same value; we will call this value a.
The equation then becomes:

$$h = \frac{(c+a)x - (b+a)y}{3y - 5x} \quad [2]$$

The values of h are equal, so we can set the right hand side of equation [1] and [2] equal:

$$\frac{cx - by}{3y - 5x} = \frac{(c+a)x - (b+a)y}{3y - 5x} \qquad \text{Equate [1] and [2].}$$

$$\qquad\qquad\qquad\qquad\qquad\qquad\quad \text{The denominators are equal so they cancel out.}$$

$$cx - by = (c+a)x - (b+a)y \qquad \text{Expand the brackets.}$$

$$cx - by = cx + ax - by - ay \qquad \text{Cancel } cx \text{ and } -by \text{ from both sides.}$$

$$0 = ax - ay \qquad \text{Add } ay.$$

$$ax = ay \qquad \text{Divide by } a.$$

$$x = y$$

Since x and y are equal the required ratio will be $x : y = 1 : 1$

6

We need to compare the combined factory outputs to answer this question.
When comparing values the units should be consistent.
In this case the aircraft production is defined as build time per aircraft.
This is not consistent, but if we define the production as aircraft per week, then the units will be consistent.
Factory A completes 1 aircraft every 8 weeks, which is the same as $\frac{1}{8}$ aircraft per week.

Factory B completes 1 aircraft every 12 weeks, which is the same as $\frac{1}{12}$ aircraft per week.

Factory C completes 1 aircraft every 6 weeks, which is the same as $\frac{1}{6}$ aircraft per week.

We now combine factory A and C:
$\frac{1}{8} + \frac{1}{6} = \frac{7}{24}$ air craft per week.
This means it takes $\frac{24}{7}$ weeks for factory A and C to complete one aircraft.

We now combine factory A and B:
$\frac{1}{8} + \frac{1}{12} = \frac{5}{24}$ air craft per week.
This means it takes $\frac{24}{5}$ weeks for factory A and B to complete one aircraft.

The difference in time to produce an aircraft will be $\frac{24}{5} - \frac{24}{7} = \frac{48}{35}$ weeks.

The answer must be in days, so we multiply by 7: $\frac{48}{35} \times 7 = \frac{48}{5}$ or 9.6 days.

The correct answer is $\frac{48}{5}$ or 9.6 days quicker.

7

We need to compare the combined pipe outputs to answer this question.

When comparing values the units should be consistent.

We can convert the units to "fraction of water tank filled per hour".

Pipe X fills the tank completely in 16 hours, which is the same as $\frac{1}{16}$ tanks per hour.

Pipe Y fills the tank completely in 30 hours, which is the same as $\frac{1}{30}$ tanks per hour.

Pipe Z empties the tank completely in x hours, which is the same as $-\frac{1}{x}$ tanks per hour.

The negative is used here because pipe Z empties the tank and we need to combine all the effects of the pipes.

We know that when all three pipes are operating the tank fills up in 80 hours.

The collective effect is to say the tank fills at a rate of $\frac{1}{80}$ tanks per hour.

We now have the basis for an equation to solve for x:

$$\frac{1}{16} + \frac{1}{30} - \frac{1}{x} = \frac{1}{80}$$

Pipe X and pipe Y fill the tank, so they have positive values.

Pipe Z empties the tank, so this is negative.

$$\frac{23}{240} - \frac{1}{x} = \frac{1}{80}$$

$$\frac{1}{16} + \frac{1}{30} = \frac{23}{240}$$

$$\frac{23x - 240}{240x} = \frac{1}{80}$$

$$\frac{23}{240} - \frac{1}{x} = \frac{23x - 240}{240x}$$

$$\frac{23x - 240}{3x} = 1$$

Multiply by 80.

$$23x - 240 = 3x$$

Multiply by $3x$.

$$20x = 240$$

Subtract $3x$ and add 240.

$$x = 12$$

Divide by 20.

The correct answer is $x = 12$.

It takes pipe Z 12 hours to empty the tank on its own.

8

The mean of a group of values is found by:

$$\text{mean} = \frac{\text{sum of values}}{\text{number of values}}$$

The mean of the reciprocal of the values is required.

The reciprocal flips a fraction around, so the reciprocal of $\frac{2}{3}$ is $\frac{3}{2}$.

The values given are a, b and c.

Their reciprocals will be $\frac{1}{a}, \frac{1}{b}$ and $\frac{1}{c}$ respectively.

The mean of these three is $\frac{1}{8}$.

If we were to form an equation at this stage we would have all three unknowns in one equation when we really require one unknown.

We are told b is three times a: so $b = 3a$.

We are told c is two times b: so $c = 6a$.

We can now form the equation:

$$\frac{\frac{1}{a}+\frac{1}{3a}+\frac{1}{6a}}{3}=\frac{1}{8}$$

Form an equation based on the mean calculation.

$$\frac{1}{a}+\frac{1}{3a}+\frac{1}{6a}=\frac{3}{8}$$

Multiply by 3.

$$1+\frac{1}{3}+\frac{1}{6}=\frac{3a}{8}$$

Multiply by a.

$$1+\frac{1}{3}+\frac{1}{6}=\frac{3}{2}$$

$$\frac{3}{2}=\frac{3a}{8}$$

Divide by 3.

$$\frac{1}{2}=\frac{a}{8}$$

Multiply by 8.

$$a=4$$

$$b=3a$$
$$=12$$
$$c=2b$$
$$=24$$

The correct answers are $a=4, b=12$ and $c=24$.

9

An integer can be written as the product of two integers in addition to a remainder.

We are told that when the integer x is divided by 6 the remainder is 5.

From this statement we can say that 6 goes into x an undefined number of times and the remainder will be 5.

Let a be the number of times that 6 goes into x (a is an integer).

From this we can write:

$$\frac{x}{6}=a \text{ remainder } 5$$

And so

$$x=6a+5$$

We can also find an expression for x^2:

$$x^2=(6a+5)^2$$
$$=(6a+5)(6a+5)$$
$$=36a^2+30a+30a+25$$
$$=36a^2+60a+25$$

Now we can consider what happens when we divide x^2 by 6:

$$\frac{x^2}{6}=\frac{36a^2+60a+25}{6}$$
$$=6a^2+10a+\frac{25}{6}$$

Now $6a^2$ and $10a$ are both whole numbers, but $\frac{25}{6}$ is not.

It is this term that determines the remainder.

$$\frac{25}{6}=4 \text{ remainder } 1$$

The remainder when x^2 is divided by 6 is 1.

10

We need to form equations that link the number of tiles that cover the bathroom and the area of both the tiles and the bathroom.

The small tile has length to width ratio 4 : 3

We can let the actual lengths of the small tile be $4x : 3x$ where x is a multiplier that gives the correct values.

We know n of these tiles are required to cover the bathroom.

The area of each of the small tiles will be $4x \times 3x = 12x^2$.

We can form the first equation:

$$\frac{86400}{12x^2} = n \quad [1]$$

The large tile has length to width ratio 6 : 5

We can let the actual lengths of the large tile be $6y : 5y$ where y is a multiplier that gives the correct values.

We know $n - 20$ of these tiles are required to cover the bathroom.

The area of each of the large tiles will be $6y \times 5y = 30y^2$.

We can form the second equation:

$$\frac{86400}{30y^2} = n - 20 \quad [2]$$

We also know that the large tile has an area 48cm^2 greater than the small tile, from which we can write a third equation:

$$30y^2 = 12x^2 + 48 \quad [3]$$

Our objective is to find n. We need to eliminate y and then x to get an equation containing n only.

Start by replacing $30y^2$ in [2] by $12x^2 + 48$ in [3]:

$$\frac{86400}{30y^2} = n - 20$$

$$\frac{86400}{12x^2 + 48} = n - 20 \quad [4]$$

If we rearrange [1] to make $12x^2$ the subject we obtain:

$$\frac{86400}{12x^2} = n$$

$$86400 = 12nx^2$$

$$12x^2 = \frac{86400}{n}$$

Now we substitute this value into [4]:

$$\frac{86400}{12x^2 + 48} = n - 20 \qquad \text{Replace } 12x^2 \text{ with } \frac{86400}{n}.$$

$$\frac{86400}{\frac{86400}{n} + 48} = n - 20$$

$$\frac{86400n}{86400 + 48n} = n - 20 \qquad \text{Multiply each term in the fraction by } n.$$

$$\frac{1800n}{1800 + n} = n - 20 \qquad \begin{array}{l}\text{Divide each term in the fraction by 48.}\\ \text{Multiply by } (1800 + n).\end{array}$$

$$1800n = (n + 1800)(n - 20) \qquad \text{Expand the brackets on the right hand side.}$$

$$1800n = n^2 - 20n + 1800n - 36000 \qquad \begin{array}{l}\text{Collect all the terms on one side so that the quadratic is}\\ \text{set equal to zero.}\end{array}$$

$$1800n = n^2 + 1780n - 36000$$

$$n^2 - 20n - 36000 = 0 \qquad \text{Factorise.}$$

$$(n - 200)(n + 180) = 0 \qquad \text{Reject the negative solution.}$$

n is positive so $n = 200$ is the correct answer.

ABOUT THE AUTHOR

Barton Maths Tuition provides educational texts for GCSE students. The author is a private maths and science tutor supporting students in the area around Barton Under Needwood, Staffordshire.

18572607R00070

Printed in Great Britain
by Amazon